Ethics and the Old Testament

Ethics and the Old Testament

John Barton

The 1997 Diocese of British Columbia
John Albert Hall Lectures
at the
Centre for Studies in Religion and Society
in the University of Victoria

Trinity Press International
Harrisburg, Pennsylvania

Library of Congress Cataloging-in-Publication Data
Barton, John, 1948–
Ethics and the Old Testament / John Barton. —
1st North American ed.
p. cm.
"The 1997 Diocese of British Columbia John Albert
Hall lectures at the Centre for Studies in Religion and
Society in the University of Victoria."
Includes bibliographical references.
ISBN 1-56338-234-2
1. Ethics in the Bible. 2. Bible. O.T.—Criticism,
interpretation, etc. I. University of Victoria (B.C.).
Centre for Studies in Religion and Society. II. Title.
BS1199.E8B37 1998
241.5—dc21 97–45168
CIP

First North American Edition 1998
by Trinity Press International
P.O. Box 1321
Harrisburg, PA 17112

Trinity Press International is part
of the Morehouse Group.
Printed in Great Britain

FOR KATIE

THE JOHN ALBERT HALL LECTURES

Churchman, chemist, pioneer, soldier, businessman and philanthropist, John Albert Hall (1869–1933) emigrated from Britain to Canada in the last decade of the nineteenth century and made his home in Victoria, British Columbia. He left a legacy to the Diocese of British Columbia to found a lectureship to stimulate harmony between the Christian religion and contemporary thought. Colonel Hall's generosity sustained the work of three successive Canon Lecturers: Michael Coleman, Hilary Butler and Thomas Bailey. It also helped found the Greater Victoria Lay School of Theology. Since 1995 it has been supporting the lectureship's partnership between the Diocese of British Columbia and the University of Victoria's Centre for Studies in Religion and Society.

The Centre was established in 1991 to foster the scholarly study of religion in relation to the sciences, ethics, social and economic development, and other aspects of culture. As Co-sponsor of the John Albert Hall Lecture Series it assists in the fulfilment of the terms of the trust.

John Albert Hall lecturers are outstanding Christian theologians who address themselves to the church, the university and the community during a two-week Fellowship in Victoria, Canada. Publication of these lectures allows a wider audience to benefit from both the lecture series and the work of the Centre.

Contents

Foreword

This book is a slightly lengthened form of the John Albert Hall Lectures for 1997, which I delivered in January and February 1997 at the kind invitation of the Educational Trusts Board of the Diocese of British Columbia. The Diocese collaborated with the Centre for Studies in Religion and Society of the University of Victoria, so that some lectures were given in the Centre and others in Christ Church Cathedral, Victoria. It is a great pleasure to have this opportunity to thank the many people who welcomed my wife and me to Victoria, and above all Michael Hadley, at that time Acting Director of the Centre, and Anita Borradaile Hadley, for much generous hospitality.

Since my return to Oxford I have delivered the lectures as a short course for theology undergraduates, and some of the modifications to the original text results from helpful comments made by them – and also to particularly constructive comment by David Reimer, which I am glad to acknowledge.

There is always a risk in presenting a highly technical and much-researched field for a non-specialist audience, but at the same time it is vital to do so if one is to avoid merely talking to oneself. The audiences to which I spoke in Victoria made many acute observations, and helped me to understand my own subject better, and I am most grateful to them.

This book is dedicated with much love to my daughter Katie.

John Barton
Oxford, July 1997

I

The Vitality of
Old Testament Ethics

'It is difficult for those who read the Bible regularly to realize how strange it looks to the outside world.'[1] Very often the book which to Christians, who are familiar with it, seems a comfort and an inspiration strikes others as thoroughly barbaric and alien; it seems to come from a world so remote from our own that it can have nothing to say to us. This is perhaps nowhere so obvious as when we speak of the Bible as a resource for Christian ethics. There is nothing easier than to produce a list of reasons why the ethicist might want to ignore the Old Testament in particular. Old Testament law lays down the death penalty for adultery (Lev. 20.10, Deut. 22.22), appears to envisage mutilation as a punishment for assault ('an eye for an eye . . .', Ex. 21.23–4, Lev. 24.19–20; Deut. 19.21), forbids the taking of interest on loans (Deut. 23.19), which would cause severe difficulties to modern economies, and treats those with various skin diseases – *sara'at*, traditionally translated 'leprosy' – as social and religious outcasts (Lev. 13–14). And the law is only part of the story. The book of Joshua reports with approval the massacre of the inhabitants of whole cities by the Israelites as they strengthened their hold on the Promised Land (Josh. 6, 11); while Saul, the first king of Israel, loses divine approval because he is not sufficently zealous in carrying out God's command to annihilate everything that breathes when he defeats the Amalekites. The prophet Samuel finishes the job for him: 'Samuel said to Agag [the Amalekite king, whom Saul had spared], "As your sword has made women childless, so shall your mother be childless among women." And Samuel hewed Agag in pieces before the LORD in Gilgal' (I Sam. 15.33).

I begin on this unpleasant note because I think it is important to acknowledge at the outset that establishing the relevance of Old Testament ethics to life today is an uphill task. For some Christians the felt claim of the Old Testament as scripture means that it seems natural to them to accept even the ethical implications of the unappealing passages I've just mentioned, and to find some way of accommodating them into a coherent moral system by which to live in the late twentieth century. But for many more Christians, and for all who have no religious commitment, this seems implausible at best and ridiculous or even immoral at worst. To such people it will probably seem that a book on the relation between the Old Testament and Christian ethics is doomed from the outset, a *tour de force* whose object is to explain away laws and customs that ought to be abhorrent to every reasonable person.

That is not my intention, and explaining away is not on my agenda. I want to show that in many areas of ethical enquiry the Old Testament has much to teach us, but I shall not make any attempt to smooth over the blemishes which anyone today is bound to see in it. Indeed, I want to begin not with the more obviously appealing aspects of Old Testament literature which are sometimes used as a smokescreen to hide the elements of blood and thunder, but with a few other, and more general, features that make the Old Testament even harder to use today than its secular critics realize. But I hope by that apparently unpromising route to arrive at a more fruitful way of approaching the Old Testament as a possible resource for our own ethical thinking.

The Old Testament text that has had the widest currency as a summary of the ethical conduct demanded by God is the Ten Commandments or Decalogue. The Commandments are often displayed on the walls of synagogues and of churches to remind worshippers of the moral code they are committed to. Here is the text as it appears in Ex. 20.1–17 (there is a less familiar version in Deut. 5.6–21):

And God spoke all these words, saying, 'I am the LORD your God, who brought you out of the land of Egypt, out of the house of bondage. You shall have no other gods before me. You shall not make for yourself a graven image, or any likeness of anything that is in heaven above, or that is in the earth beneath, or that is in the water under the earth; you shall not bow down to them or serve them; for I the LORD your God am a jealous God, visiting the iniquity of the fathers upon the children to the third and the fourth generation of those who hate me, but showing steadfast love to thousands of those who love me and keep my commandments.

You shall not take the name of the LORD your God in vain; for the LORD will not hold him guiltless who takes his name in vain.

Remember the sabbath day, to keep it holy. Six days you shall labour, and do all your work; but the seventh day is a sabbath to the LORD your God; in it you shall not do any work, you, or your son, or your daughter, your manservant, or your maidservant, or your cattle, or the sojourner who is within your gates; for in six days the LORD made heaven and earth, the sea, and all that is in them, and rested the seventh day; therefore the LORD blessed the sabbath day and hallowed it.

Honour your father and your mother, that your days may be long in the land which the LORD your God gives you. You shall not kill. You shall not commit adultery. You shall not steal. You shall not bear false witness against your neighbour. You shall not covet your neighbour's house; you shall not covet your neighbour's wife, or his manservant, or his maidservant, or his ox, or his ass, or anything that is your neighbour's.'

If inspected closely the Commandments turn out to be much more limited in appeal than they seem at first sight. One of the effects of biblical criticism is always to locate texts more precisely in their historical and social context, and if we do this with the Commandments we find that they are more time-bound than Jews and Christians have thought them. The easiest way to show this is to ask who is being addressed in this text. Well, the person in question has a house, a wife, and servants, and so has his neighbour. He is competent to give evidence in court and consequently needs to be warned not to give false evidence. He has a father and mother who need to be looked after. He is, in short, a free adult male of the property-owning class, with a household and an extended family – broadly speaking the kind of person who had the vote in most Western democracies a century ago. The Decalogue does not tell us anything about the moral rights or duties of women, or children, or slaves, but only about those of the people who ran Israelite society in the period before the Exile of the sixth century BC: it is addressed to free men.

If we find some of the actual moral injunctions in various parts of the Old Testament rather scandalous, we should see that some of the underlying assumptions are also scandalous from a modern perspective. A historical assessment of the Ten Commandments has the effect of distancing them from us and in the process making them seem rather alien. When I hear appeals for society to get back to the Ten Commandments, I find myself wanting, perhaps rather mischievously, to ask whether we actually want to reintroduce the kind of society within which they make sense – what we would call, loosely, a patriarchal society. Of course there are all sorts of ways of trying to generalize from the specifics of the Commandments; but on the face of it, taken 'literally', they reflect a situation radically different from our own.

The specific social location of Old Testament texts, then, is likely in general to be a problem for the ethicist. Equally difficult is the huge *variety* of ethical commitments and points of view represented in the Old Testament text. This is scarcely surprising in a collection of writings spanning perhaps a millennium, but it certainly does make the material slippery to handle. On some ethical issues there are diametrically opposed positions within contemporary books. One of the best-known examples would be the question of the correct stance that Jews ought to adopt to foreigners. The books of Ezra and Nehemiah insist that intermarriage, and a concomitant relaxed attitude to non-Jews, are wholly unacceptable – Nehemiah tells us how he pulled out the hair of some people who had intermarried with foreigners (Neh. 13.23–7); whereas the book of Ruth, a product of the same period – probably the fifth or fourth century BC – praises the Moabite woman Ruth who marries an Israelite and becomes the ancestor of King David himself. Anyone who wants to treat the biblical text as an absolute authority will have problems in deciding which line of thought is to be followed in this matter.

Thirdly, texts that deal with ethical issues often operate with categories that simply do not make sense within the moral universe most of us inhabit. I mentioned the treatment of people with 'leprosy', but this is only one example of a wider problem. Old Testament thinking about sickness and health operates with notions of ritual purity which find no place in most modern ethical systems. There are parallels in modern thinking to the Old Testament idea of purity, which I want to explore later in this book, but they do not on the whole find their way into our ethical codes – they operate at a more informal level in our culture, and we would normally distinguish them from morality, a realm where intention and guilt, rather than objective 'pollution' or 'defilement', are the key concepts. But a great deal of what the Old Testament has to say about morality presupposes concepts of purity and impurity, and if our thinking about ethics is to take Old Testament material seriously, rather than simply dipping into it where it seems attractive and readily usable, it needs to come to terms with the difficulty this raises.

So the initial difficulty of the proverbially bloodthirsty nature of Old Testament morality turns out to be almost the least of our troubles. Much more troublesome are the Old Testament's rootedness in a culture which is not ours, its internal contradictions, and its use of categories of thought which are alien to modern thinking about morality. All these things mean that there can surely be no simple route from the ethics of the Old Testament to anything we might be able to say about moral questions.

Some people might say at this point, 'What did you expect? Anyone who wasn't blinded by the religious status this very curious set of texts has within Judaism and Christianity would see it as fairly obvious that they have little to contribute to modern ethical thought. Religious people are interested in them because they are their holy scriptures, but for the rest of us they are really pretty dead wood by now.' But this is a point I would not accept. Among texts from past cultures some are simply dated, and a dialogue with them is impossible. But others survive because they have been found by successive generations to illuminate the human condition, and for that reason we keep coming back to them and never exhaust their meaning. Such, for example, are the tragedies of classical Greece. Ancient Greek society is every bit as remote from us as most of the societies whose thinking finds expression in the Old Testament; but no one doubts that the values enshrined in the classical tragedies can illuminate our own lives, which is why we still perform them. My claim for the Old Testament is no higher than this: I am making no appeal to its status as the scriptures of Jews and Christians, but approaching it simply as an ancient text. But my contention will be that this ancient text does, contrary to one's first impressions, have something to say about humanity and its ethical norms which can continue to resonate in our own, very different culture.

To show this we may go back to the three examples just discussed of how alien the Old Testament is, because they are equally good examples of how much it still has to say. The Ten Commandments are, just as I argued, the expression of the values of a particular type of society in one period of the history of Israel, probably (I would guess) in the eighth or seventh century BC, the age of the great prophets, Amos, Isaiah, and Jeremiah. When general conclusions are drawn from them, and they are treated as if they applied in the same way to a society such as our own, their particularity is being to some extent eroded, and we are seeing them as it were through a soft focus. However, if we try to read them in their own context and against their own society we shall quickly find that they make sense only against a complex background of ethical assumptions and practices many of which turn out to be more widely applicable than we might have expected.

What assumptions hold the Ten Commandments together? Christians and Jews have always pointed to the existence of two 'tables' in the Commandments, conventionally thought of as the contents of the two tablets of stone which Moses brought down from Mount Sinai. The two tables contain, somewhat asymmetrically, duties to

God (four) and duties to fellow human beings (six). But it is important to see that the two tables are not separated within the text, and it seems clear that the society in which the Commandments were first formulated thought of the two types of legislation as binding in exactly the same way. This is therefore a somewhat theocratic society, where proper observance of direct duties towards God in terms of cultic loyalty and devotion is seen as being in the same class as moral obligations towards others. All the evidence we have suggests that Israel in the period of the kings (say roughly 900–600 BC) was indeed such a society. This does not mean that people were more 'religious' than at other times, if we mean by 'religious' pious or God-fearing or spiritual. But it does mean that religion had not been, as people sometimes say it has in our day, 'privatized'. Religious observance was a matter of public performance and publicly-acknowledged obligation alongside obligations towards fellow human beings.

The second table of the Decalogue is remarkable for the terse way in which it handles three major offences: theft, murder, and adultery. Though Exodus presents these, like all the other laws, as directly revealed by God, from a historical point of view we have to note that all the societies of the ancient Near East had legislation – sometimes fairly brutal legislation – against these three crimes. The Decalogue is unusual in treating them in such a generalized way. Though other legislation in the Pentateuch qualifies what is said here by allowing for difficult and uncertain cases, a society which produces such categorical formulations is presumably very clear about its basic principles. Like everything else in the Ten Commandments, I assume that these laws rest on a very ancient consensus about respect for life and property, though it's probable that the prohibition of adultery was understood as a subset of the law about theft, with the wife being seen first as her husband's property. Even if this is so, the two laws are distinct, and there is much evidence that in historical times wives were seen as much more than property, although relations between the sexes never became fully symmetrical, any more than they did in other ancient societies (or most modern ones for that matter).

The Decalogue ends with the most puzzling Commandment of all, the prohibition of coveting. Christians are so used to treating the Commandments rather metaphorically – taking the law against murder as a warning about the sinfulness of anger, for example – that it seems natural to them that there should be an exhortation not to be envious and greedy. But if we think of this as a text with a real social setting, and one in which the sins or crimes condemned are perfectly literal, then the Tenth Commandment becomes quite an oddity. Short of employing George Orwell's thought police, one can hardly make covetousness a crime, since it cannot be detected or demonstrated. It's not surprising that some scholars have proposed that the verb here (*ḥamad*) means 'to attempt to steal' – covetousness externalized, as it were. But it never means that elsewhere in the Bible, and I think we have to accept that the Ten Commandments really do contain a prohibition of having a wrong mental attitude. This perhaps implies in turn that the Commandments did not originally function as a law *code*, but were more in the nature of teaching or instruction than of enforceable legislation.

And that may free us to consider what might be called the social vision undergirding the Commandments. However much or little they may have constituted a real legal code, they are certainly an expression of a particular consensus about the nature of ethical obligation in society. This obligation, which extends at least to those who have a stake in the way society is ordered, embraces three realms: proper piety towards God, due respect to one's neighbour and everything that is an extension of one's neighbour, and a generous and ungrudging attitude towards others. As we have seen, the person addressed by the Commandments is the free adult male Israelite, and nothing I can say will avoid what we'd now call the sexism and racism inherent in that. But, to present the matter in a positive light, the Commandments at least imply that the men to whom they are addressed recognize clear limits to their own autonomy, and see the good life as one lived in community in an atmosphere of mutual respect and toleration, not encroaching on each other's legitimate spheres. They also acknowledge considerable obligations towards God, and have already accepted the principle which the prophets spent a lot of time in insisting on, that the God of Israel had exclusive rights within Israel and must not be worshipped alongside any other divine beings.

None of these matters, taken individually, was unique to Israel. All of the nations in the ancient Near East had laws forbidding murder, theft, and adultery; all of them had assumptions about how the gods were to be worshipped, though these differed of course in implying polytheism; and all had teachings of sages which deplored attitudes such as anger, pride, and covetousness. The unusual aspect of the Ten Commandments is that these three sorts of ethical material are presented in a single text, as part of a unified vision of how to live well. Many details of Israel's ethical programme are paralleled elsewhere, and some details strike us as abhorrent; but the drive to unify and reconcile all parts of that programme and bring them under a single umbrella as parts of life lived before God remains impressive, and unusual.

If we move on to the second problematic feature of Old Testament ethics, its internal inconsistencies, we can again understand what is going on better if we take a rather longer view. On the issue I took as my example, the attitude of Jews after the Babylonian Exile towards foreigners, there is indeed a stark opposition. While Nehemiah is tearing out the hair of men who married foreign wives, the prophet who wrote the third part of the book of Isaiah is writing, 'The foreigners who join themselves to the LORD, to minister to him, to love the name of the LORD, and to be his servants ... these will I bring to my holy mountain, and make them joyful in my house of prayer . . . for my house shall be called a house of prayer for all peoples' (Isa. 56.6–7). These positions cannot be reconciled. But if we try to look behind them, we might say that they are opposite responses to a shared ethical agenda. Trito-Isaiah, as the author of Isa. 56–66 is generally known, did not believe that the question of who belongs to the holy people was unimportant, any more than Nehemiah did. Trito-Isaiah thought membership should be open to all, Nehemiah that it was to be determined entirely by physical descent. But there is no question about the concept of membership, in itself: neither was saying simply that there was no chosen people, that it did not matter whether someone was a Jew or not.

In the same way it is possible to see many of the disagreements between different Old Testament texts over ethical matters as differences of opinion within a shared framework of assumptions. To take another striking dissonance: the author of Kings praised Jehu for his extremely bloody coup against the house of king Ahab (see II Kings 10), whereas the prophet Hosea (Hos. 1.4–5) regarded it as a terrible sin. Both agreed, however, that dynasties like Ahab's were an abomination, because they had breached the commandment to worship only Yahweh, the God of Israel. The difference was over the practical question of what should be done about such kings. And, in general, we may say that there is an extraordinary agreement among Old Testament writers about what constitutes, as I just called it, the moral agenda.

Thirdly, there are the various moral categories which are common in the Old Testament but alien, for the most part, to us today. We soon become aware that we are reading a text from an ancient culture whose whole understanding of reality is significantly different from ours. I instanced ideas about pollution and purity as particularly salient examples of this. I shall return to these ideas later, and try to suggest that they are in fact rather less alien than they seem at first. Nevertheless, when Old Testament writers assume that there is a property called uncleanness or pollution that is conveyed equally by unlawful killing, mistakes in the offering of sacrifice, and menstruation, we know that we are in an unfamiliar world. At this point, however, we need to enlarge our own horizons somewhat, and to remember that ancient Israel's concern with purity did not die out with the world of antiquity, but survived in a robust form to become part of the type of Judaism which we know today as 'Orthodox'. Christians are notorious with Jews for their tendency to describe, as though they had long ago ceased to exist, customs which are still alive and well in the life of the synagogue around the corner. I shall be suggesting in due course that the system of clean and unclean in Judaism can be helpful to the Christian ethicist in dealing with certain moral concerns which are a great preoccupation of twentieth-century Christian morality but have proved curiously intractable within traditional Christian, and Western, moral categories – one of these being the debate about ecology.

My claim for Old Testament ethics is thus that it is more unified, more subtle, and more relevant to our own concerns than it appears at first sight. This can only be shown, of course, through specific examples, and I hope to provide the demonstration in the course of the rest of this book. What we might note at this point, however, is a certain paradox which will prove illuminating as we proceed. What I have been saying up to this point could be summarized as the claim that Old Testament ethics forms more of a coherent system than modern Western people are apt to assume. Moral propositions and norms in the Old Testament are not random shots in the dark, but parts of a reasonably unified moral programme. The paradox is that this programme is seldom expressed through the kinds of generalizations or statements of principle that we look for in Western moral philosophy. Our first impression, that the Old Testament presents its morality unsystematically and through a variety of vehicles, none of them much like the way we write about ethics, is misleading if it encourages us to think that it is just a muddle. But it is perfectly accurate in so far as it reminds us that the biblical way of conveying moral truth is always through the particular and the specific. Old Testament writers are maddeningly unsystematic. Asked for a general statement of moral principle, they reply with a little rule about local legal procedures, a story about obscure people of dubious moral character, or a hymn extolling some virtue in God with which human beings are supposed somehow to conform. Knowledge of the good for humankind lies through the observation of particulars, if Old Testament writers are to be believed.

At first sight, this is another factor separating us from them; for thinking about ethics today normally proceeds by discussing matters of general principle, and then applying these to individual cases, not the other way around. However, that is not the whole story. In the next lecture I shall be drawing extensively on the work of Martha C. Nussbaum, who has pioneered an approach to moral philosophy which begins with particularity and, even if it then goes on to think about general principles, always returns to the particular and the individual as the real stuff of moral discernment. Nussbaum began this line of investigation in her first book, *The Fragility of Goodness*,[2] in which Greek tragedy serves as the material for moral enquiry – in that case for enquiry into the relation of human intention and chance in the moral life. She took the theme further in *Love's Knowledge*,[3] where the tragedians are joined by modern novelists and poets. She sees her approach as essentially Aristotelian, sharply contrasting with a Platonic interest in universals:

> Practical wisdom [of which for Aristotle ethics forms a part] . . . uses rules only as summaries and guides; it must itself be flexible, ready for surprise, prepared to see, resourceful at improvisation. This being so, Aristotle stresses that the crucial prerequisite for practical wisdom is a long experience of life that yields an ability to understand and grasp the salient features, the practical meaning, of the concrete particulars. This sort of insight is altogether different from a deductive scientific knowledge, and is, he reminds us, more akin to sense-perception. . . . Practical insight is like perceiving in the sense that it is non-inferential, non-deductive; it is, centrally, the ability to recognize, acknowledge, respond to, pick out certain salient features of a complex situation. And just as the theoretical *nous* comes only out of a long experience with first principles and a sense, gained gradually in and through experience, of the fundamental role played by these principles in discourse and explanation, so too practical perception, which Aristotle also calls *nous*, is gained only through a long process of living and choosing that develops the agent's resourcefulness and responsiveness: '. . . Young people can become mathematicians and geometers and wise in things of that sort; but they do not appear to become people of practical wisdom. The reason is that practical wisdom is of the particular, which becomes graspable through experience, but a young person is not experienced. For a quantity of time is required for experience' (1142a12–16).[4]

Nussbaum has not to my knowledge commented on the ethical material in the Hebrew Bible, but it occurs to me as an Old Testament specialist that her key could indeed be turned in that lock. The Old Testament, as I have argued, usually works from particular to general, and hardly ever enunciates any principles that would strike us as universal: even such general texts as the Ten Commandments turn out to be very strongly anchored in the concerns of a particular society at a particular time, and the Ten Commandments, after all, are about as general as Hebrew moral teaching ever gets. Most Old Testament material is extremely particular and specific. But if Nussbaum is right, that may make it just the kind of material from which vital moral insight is to be gained. I shall try to show how that might be done in the next two chapters.

So far, then, I have tried to move from the difficulties anyone today is likely to find in the Old Testament as a possible source for ethics to an appreciation of where its own peculiar genius lies. Its material is time-bound, sometimes inconsistent, sometimes alien to us in its underlying assumptions. These apparent, or real, weaknesses, however, could turn out to be also its strengths. In the Old Testament we are presented, not with a carefully worked-out code allegedly valid for all time, but with a way of handling life as it presented itself in all its brokenness and particularity in the societies which formed these texts as we now have them. The Old Testament is not the stuff of which moral philosophy, as we've come to know it in the West, is made. Yet, if Martha Nussbaum is correct in her description of Aristotle's understanding of ethics, this tradition of moral philosophy itself has foundations which

17

rest on a considerable concern for particularity. Aristotle's description of the wise ethical judge, who needs maturity and a practical knowledge of the particularities of many human lives, not just an abstract knowledge of moral theory, is not so far from the 'wise man' described in the Old Testament book of Proverbs and in similar works from other pre-philosophical cultures. For such a person ethical insight is the distillation of experience – of course, experience reflected on in the light of general principles, but not simply a consideration of those principles in the absence of an encounter with the realities of life. Old Testament literature, like the Jewish rabbinic literature that is its successor, is apt to be irritating to anyone with a training in moral philosophy because of its frequent refusal to generalize. But if Nussbaum is right we might be able to make a virtue of this; perhaps it is, after all, quite a good way of approaching the complexities of human moral conduct. In the next chapter I shall try to illustrate the point by considering one central narrative text from the Old Testament, the story of David and his children.

2

Ethics and Story

'Nathan said to David, "You are the man."' These words are the climax of one of the Old Testament's most disturbing stories, the story of king David's affair with Bathsheba, the wife of one of his army officers (II Sam. 11–12). David, we are told, saw Bathsheba bathing as he walked one hot afternoon on the roof of his palace, and sent for her. After they had slept together, Bathsheba discovered that she was pregnant, and David tried various ruses to cover up what he had done, summoning her husband Uriah back from the front and trying every means to persuade him to go and spend the night at home, so that the child might appear to be his. But Uriah steadfastly refused, citing the rule that soldiers on active service must live apart from their wives. So David arranged for Uriah to be placed where the fighting was fiercest, and he was duly killed. Bathsheba became David's wife, and in due course the mother of Solomon, David's successor. But her first child by David died, and we are told that this was a punishment for David's sin. The prophet Nathan came to him soon after he had married Bathsheba, and told him a little parable, presented as a true story, about a rich man who was too mean to use one of his many sheep to make a meal for an unexpected visitor but instead stole the only lamb belonging to his poor neighbour. When David became angry and insisted that such a person did not deserve to live, Nathan replied simply, 'You are the man' – and foretold the death of the child born of David's adultery with Bathsheba, even though he declared that David would thereafter be forgiven because he was repentant.

In my first chapter I spoke of the ethics of the Old Testament primarily as seen in the laws which are promulgated for the life of the ancient Israelites, and especially in the Ten Commandments. But I went on to suggest that concentration on law does not do justice to what the Old Testament has to say about ethical questions, and in particular that it overlooks the many ways in which the Old Testament concentrates not on general principles but on specific cases. About half of the Old Testament, after all, consists not of overt moral teachings but of narrative: histories, legends, stories, whatever we want to call it. And narrative is necessarily particular, concerned with connected chains of actions and events which always befall particular people. What is more, Old Testament narrative seldom consists of edifying tales with an obvious moral, like Aesop's fables; usually the stories it tells resist reduction to a simple moral, or 'point'. They are not the kind of stories which we can throw away once we have extracted the meaning. They invite reading and re-reading, pondering over and revisiting. In short, most of them are literature, not just sermon examples or anecdotes.

The suggestion that narrative texts can be fruitful for ethics has come from two sources in recent years. One important contribution, about which I shall not say very much, has come from Stanley Hauerwas.[1] Hauerwas has proposed a theory of narrative ethics, in which attention to the narrative texts of the Bible – especially of the New Testament – tends to take the place of traditional moral philosophy or Christian ethics. Hauerwas' approach, to simplify it greatly for our present purposes, involves reading biblical narrative in such a way that we come to appreciate its narrative shape, the 'plot' of the story it tells, so to speak, and then lay this narrative shape alongside the shape of our own lives, the pattern they form or can form, with God's help. The narrative of the life of Jesus, supremely, has ethical authority for the Christian, and what this means is that the Christian community (and individuals within it) needs to see its life as modelled on the life of Jesus as the Gospels (collectively) portray it. Other patterns which can be fruitful for the Christian are the Old Testament pattern of the liberation from Egypt, and the giving of the Promised Land; and the life of the early church, as we find it told in Acts. The ethical ideal for the Christian is not so much to observe certain laws or commandments – Hauerwas shares the Protestant tradition which is severely doubtful of people's capacity to do that – but to imitate the narrative patterns that we find in Scripture; indeed, the idea of the imitation of Christ is closer to his ethical model than is obedience to laws.

I shall not say much more about Hauerwas, however, not because I think his system bad – on the contrary, it is a subtle and helpful way of thinking about the Christian moral life – but because it treats narrative texts in a way very different from what comes naturally to me, as a biblical specialist rather than an ethicist. It seems in some ways to sideline what for me is the chief interest of biblical (especially Old Testament) narrative, and that is its particularity. Hauerwas' approach invites us to generalize from the narratives we read, and to extract from them the basic framework that holds them together. It is not the story of Jesus in this or that Gospel, but the basic narrative outline that underlies all the Gospels, that interests him; not the individual details of the stories in Exodus or Numbers, but the basic structure of the Exodus story. While admiring this way of proceeding, I don't find I can make it my own, because as someone who studies the Old Testament I am constantly aware of how untidy it is, how often the 'plot' of biblical stories doesn't form much of a pattern, how specific and somehow ungeneralizable its narratives often are. And yet I do want to say that they can be fruitful for ethics, and perhaps even more fruitful for their very particularity. Can any progress be made along these lines?

In the first chapter I briefly introduced a second person who has tried to link ethical enquiry to narrative in a way that is rather more congenial to me than is Hauerwas' work: Martha Nussbaum. In her books *The Fragility of Goodness* and *Love's Knowledge*, Nussbaum puts forward an approach to ethics which avowedly owes less to the tradition of moral philosophy stemming from Plato, which is concerned with ethical universals, and more to the Aristotelian tradition with its emphasis on particulars. Ethical knowledge, for Aristotle, is not *episteme* – 'hard' or, as we might say, scientific knowledge, but practical wisdom. Assessing what is the right course of conduct in particular cases is not simply a matter of applying principles, however subtle those principles might be; it involves also attending to the irreducible particularity of the individual case. 'Among statements about conduct,' Aristotle said, 'those that are universal are more general, but the particular are more true – for action is concerned with particulars, and statements must harmonize with these' (*Nicomachean Ethics* 1107a.29–32). Nussbaum spells this out as follows:

> Rules are authoritative only insofar as they are correct; but they are correct only insofar as they do not err with regard to the particulars. And it is not possible for a simple universal formulation, intended to cover many different particulars, to achieve a high degree of correctness. . . . The law is here regarded as a summary of wise decisions. It is therefore appropriate to supplement it with new wise decisions made on the spot; and it is also appropriate to correct it where it does not correctly summarize what a good judge would do. Good judgement . . . supplies both a superior concreteness and a superior responsiveness or flexibility.[2]

A method of ethical enquiry that places so much emphasis on particulars is well adapted to take account of fictional narrative, historiography and drama. Like Dr Johnson, Nussbaum believes that biography gives us 'what comes near to us, what we can turn to use'. The record of individual lives in all their particularity may not yield general moral laws, but it can inform the moral life. With this in mind Nussbaum writes about Greek tragedy, where everything is particular and yet generations of people have felt that their own lives were somehow illuminated, more so paradoxically than by the much more general – and therefore, one would think, more universally applicable – teachings of ethicists and moral philosophers.

Nussbaum provides some worked examples of how tragedy may teach us about how to live, especially by an extended treatment of the character of Hecuba in Euripides' *Trojan Women*. What is of particular interest to me is that she concentrates less on the plot and more on the characterization, though she makes it clear that the characters do not exist except within the plot, that their individual traits are a product not only of who they are and what they are like, but also of what happens to them. She is anxious to stress that ethical character is not simply a product of one's will, as perhaps on a Kantian model, but also of accident and chance, good and bad luck. Her book is subtitled *Luck and Ethics in Greek Tragedy and Philosophy*, and the theme of luck or chance – *tyche* – is never far away. But the shape of the plot, in Hauerwas' sense, is not of primary interest to her.[3] What concerns her is the interplay of character with event. The protagonists in tragedies are brought low by a mixture of their own mistakes, the malice of others, and the impersonal forces of chance, and it is through analysing all these factors that the commentator can articulate the way in which the tragedy can be fruitful for us, as we seek to discover how we ought to live in a world where the same three factors will always operate.

This is an inadequate sketch of Nussbaum's subtle arguments, but it will have to do for now, and I hope that it is enough to suggest the question whether a similar analysis of biblical narratives might also bear fruit – not because they are sacred scripture, but because, like Greek tragedies, some of them at least are profound accounts of fallible human characters caught in the interplay between other people, chance, luck, and fortune, and the perceived experience of divine intervention or providence. And for me this is nowhere clearer than in the story of David.

David's character is delineated right at the beginning of the story with extraordinary dramatic irony, given what is to follow:

> In the spring of the year, the time when kings go forth to battle, David sent Joab, and his servants with him, and all Israel; and they ravaged the Ammonites, and besieged Rabbah. But David remained at Jerusalem. And it happened, late one afternoon, when David arose from his couch and was walking upon the roof of the king's house, that he saw from the roof a woman bathing; and the woman was very beautiful (II Sam. 11.1–2).

The story is essentially all present in these opening lines. The dead, clichéd phrase about the spring as 'the time when kings go forth to battle' is given new life with deadly effect when it is followed by the news that David, so far from going forth himself, sent Joab while he stayed in Jerusalem to enjoy an afternoon nap, and to stroll on his roof, like the devil in I Peter 5.8, 'seeking someone to devour'. Nothing is said to condemn David, but after this nothing needs to be. Again, we are told nothing of the nature of his affair with Bathsheba, whether she was willing or unwilling, and whether it would have made any difference anyway. The narrator does not actually present what happens as rape, but the difference in status between David and Bathsheba suggests that her consent was not a primary concern. Consistently with this, Bathsheba is always presented in II Samuel and I Kings as a figure with no personality of her own, but as acting only on the bidding of others; it is her disastrous intervention with Solomon on behalf of Adonijah, a son of David by a different wife, that costs Adonijah the throne and his life (see I Kings 2.13–25).

Indeed, all the characters in the story are gradually drawn into some degree of connivance with David, whether they choose it or not; perhaps even the wholly innocent Uriah, Bathsheba's husband. David calls him back from the campaign against the Ammonites for no apparent reason, though really, of course, to persuade him to sleep with Bathsheba and so establish the false supposition that the child is his own; but he refuses to play, and we are never told whether he knew or not, though perhaps we are meant to think that he probably did. 'Uriah said to David, "The ark and Israel and Judah dwell in booths; and my lord Joab and the servants of my lord are camping in the open field; shall I then go to my house, to eat and to drink, *and to lie with my wife*? As you live, and as your soul lives, I will not do this thing." ' At this we say to ourselves, He's guessed; and perhaps David did the same.[4] But Uriah's virtuous refusal to connive with David issues in his own death, he himself being required to carry the orders that will lead to his death at the hands of the Ammonites. And this virtue of his is as powerful an instrument as

David's own vice in helping forward the tragic plot, for the equally innocent child born to Bathsheba is now known to be David's and dies in its turn as part of the entail of David's own guilt. David's adultery sets in train a chain of events which sweeps up innocent and guilty alike.

The prelude to this death is Nathan's parable, which I outlined earlier, and it is the only place in the story where there is a divine intervention – death from illness being seen in the culture of the time as a direct action by God or the gods, unedifyingly for us in this case, since the person who suffers is least of all to blame for what has happened. The child's death is, however, presented as a punishment on David. We expect, having heard Nathan's assurance that David will now be forgiven, that all will be well; the child's death, as it were, provides the necessary atonement for David's sin. But the author is not so simple. God does not speak directly to us in Nathan's words; God is a character in the story, and what he says is not necessarily completely true. In the subsequent events we see that David's guilt is very far from having been expunged, and it works itself out in ways for which he has no direct responsibility, yet which cannot be seen as other than tainted by his character. His son, Amnon, rapes his own sister, Tamar: of course David did nothing to cause this, yet in whose family would it be likelier to happen? The rape is avenged by another son, Absalom, who kills Amnon and gives Tamar the only recompense available in that society to unmarried victims of rape, a perpetual place in his household with neither honour nor future. But then Absalom turns against David and rebels, and in his turn dies in an ensuing battle. By the time that, as the author puts it, 'the kingdom was established in the hands of Solomon' (I Kings 2.2.46), the stage is littered with corpses, all of them arguably the responsibility of David, perhaps all of them also the responsibility of God, who like the gods in a Greek tragedy will not let David's guilt rest, and in another way many of them the result of bad luck, of being in the wrong place at the wrong time. The story does not tell us what to do, though obviously enough it might warn us not to commit adultery; rather, it poses the question, what does it mean to live in a world where guilt, innocent suffering, and bad luck mix to make a cocktail of disaster and despair? The narrator gives us no ethical laws, but he does give us a neutrally observed depiction of life in a world where there is evil and ill fortune, and invites us to contemplate it with those two Aristotelian qualities, terror and pity.

There is one essential point that needs to be made about Martha Nussbaum's approach to narrative, and that is that it is anti-relativistic. We can learn from the heroes of Greek tragedies, from the characters in the biblical stories, or from the characters in modern novels (Nussbaum's *Love's Knowledge* studies Dickens and Henry James) only if we all share a common humanity – if David, for example, belongs in some sense to our world as well as his own. The prevailing mood in many branches of the humanities today is strongly in favour of relativism. The people of the past, it is felt, do not exist in the same world as ourselves; if we choose to use old texts, we have to do so by reading them quite deliberately with our own agenda, not by trying to adjust ourselves to theirs, which in the nature of things is impossible. Nussbaum represents against this an older kind of liberalism, in which people from the past *can* communicate with us and can be recognized, just like our contemporaries, as sharing the same needs, emotions, and frailties as ourselves. I do not think the study of biblical texts will survive very long unless this general point of view is accepted; they will otherwise become, first, blank canvases on which we paint our own pictures, and then uninteresting ancient fragments not worth bothering with at all. Nussbaum's model, however, treats past writings as genuine dialogue partners for us, repositories of wisdom and insight, when they are read within their original context. Though alien to us in so many ways, they come to us from people who like us were human and had to cope with the human condition we share with them.

Indeed, she makes the startling suggestion that the reason why we can learn from the struggles and dilemmas of people in stories is not that they are real but that we ourselves are fictional.[5] What she means by this is that all our relationships are with people to whom we relate somewhat as we do to characters in fictional literature. We cannot get close to another person unless we see them as making a certain sort of sense, having a life history with something that could be called a plot, a personality with a certain Gestalt or shape to which we can relate. That is why, when we first meet someone, we directly or indirectly quiz them on who they are and where they have come from; and if we find ourselves drawn to them, we develop an intense interest in their total life history. Drawing a fictional character is an imitation of this process. But the point can easily be stood on its head, and we can say that getting to know another real person is a little like drawing a fictional character. An inability to do this is an aspect of some sorts of mental impairment, where other people present themselves to the sufferer as a random collection of unconnected emotions and drives, making no coherent sense. Fictionalizing others, in the sense intended by Nussbaum, is actually part of getting to know who they really are – constructing a profile of how they make sense.

Conversely, when we read fiction, we find (if it is good fiction) that the characters are real in rather the same sense: their characters hang together and add up to a certain kind of whole. This again is a deeply anti-relativistic point: such a line of thought is only possible if we believe that all human beings, real ones and plausible fictional ones alike, share certain common aspects of what we call human nature, have similar needs and desires and potentialities. If that idea is abandoned, then we cannot truly 'read' either fiction or the human world around us. The outcome is a kind of solipsism in human relationships in which we regard everyone as totally opaque to us, and in the reading of literature an abandonment of the idea that we can be in touch with the intentions behind texts and a consequent belief that we can do nothing but use texts as raw material for our own experiments in constructing our own world. Of course there are terrible breakdowns in mutual comprehension among people, and there is always lurking in any relationship the appalling possibility that we may turn out wholly to have misread the other person. 'You've never had any idea what I'm really like' is among the most painful things anyone can hear. But we recognize it when understanding has broken down precisely because we have experienced occasions when it didn't break down; and this is true both in real life and in our reading of stories.

Thus stories can feed our moral life by providing us with visions of how real human beings can live through various crises and trials and remain human, that is, recognizably continuous with ourselves as part of the human race. Despite the vast differences between cultures, there are certain needs that all human beings have as human beings. Beyond the biological needs obviously common to all humans, one might mention the two named by Freud, work and love. However differently such activities or states are conceptualized in different societies, there is enough experience here shared by all to make communication across cultural gaps possible and worthwhile; and our experience of fictional characters fits into the same setting. But this possibility can only exist if the common ground really is common, if the heroes we encounter in Greek tragedy or the rather unheroic figures in the narrative books of the Hebrew Bible are not just typical ancient Greeks or typical ancient Israelites but somehow also typical human beings. Nussbaum insists on this, indeed is bound to do so if her case is to stand, and I should want to insist on it too.

I have talked about the way stories can inform what I've called our 'moral life', but this expression needs more definition. It is fairly clear that we cannot readily derive moral *duties* from narrative texts. The story of David does not tell us, as a new thing, that adultery is to be avoided, or that rape and murder are forbidden; it takes our moral perceptions on these subjects as a given. For moral injunctions in the Old Testament we have to go to the law, or to the wisdom literature. It is true that anyone who did not know that adultery, rape, and murder are wrong would come away from the story of David with a clear impression that they are; but the story is not the means anyone would choose to impart this information in the first place.

But there is something narrative can do with moral truths that cannot be done through ethical injunctions, and that is to give them what might be called an existential force. The story of David contains at its heart a miniature example of how this works, which points to the fact that the story as a whole has this effect on us, the readers or listeners. When Nathan visits David, he deliberately constructs a moral case for David to adjudicate on which appears to have no relevance to David's own conduct at all: the story of the rich man who stole the poor man's only lamb. He waits until David has worked himself into an appropriate state of righteous indignation before revealing that the tale is a parable, whose real import is the theft of another man's wife *by David himself.* (In parentheses I should say that I know this may sound an offensive way of putting it, and that what David did is in our eyes an offence first and foremost against Bathsheba, an exploitation of his superior status; but there's little doubt that the Israelite author did see the most heinous part of it as what David had done to Uriah, and it is on that basis that the parable works as a genuine parallel.) With 'You are the man' the story Nathan has told breaks its frame and comes out to hit the hearer, David, full in the face.

Now this effect, it seems to me, is itself a parable for the way the whole story of David is meant to work on *us.* We read a tale of violence, sexual exploitation, betrayal, and revenge, and we find it all very interesting and even entertaining, because for some reason nothing is more soothing than stories of other people's anger and lust – hence the popularity of whodunits. But since most of us don't commit most of the sins and crimes described in II Samuel, the story is distanced from us, and it is definitely other people's misdemeanours that it concerns. But as we become aware of the essential humanity of the characters in the story, their underlying likeness to us in spite of the scale on which they sin and suffer, the tale we are reading begins to break its own frame and to illuminate the darker reaches of our own corrupt nature.

Nowhere is this clearer than when, with hindsight, we return to the beginning, wondering how the whole downward plunge into the dark got started, how such a dreadful chain of events could ever begin, and we read again the almost casual opening:

> In the spring of the year, the time when kings go forth to battle, David sent Joab, and his servants with him, and all Israel; and they ravaged the Ammonites, and besieged Rabbah. But David remained at Jerusalem. And it happened, late one afternoon, when David arose from his couch and was walking upon the roof of the king's house, that he saw from the roof a woman bathing; and the woman was very beautiful.

Just as in a Greek tragedy, the initial fault or flaw which starts the action rolling, but after which it is unstoppable, is a simple thing, perhaps not even a sin at all. The narrator may, as I suggested, be indulging in criticism of David by saying that he stayed in Jerusalem at the time when other kings went to battle; but we don't know that for certain, and at the beginning of the story it does not seem significant. And there is really no reason why David should not stroll on his own roof in the afternoon; and no reason either, if he happened to catch sight of someone bathing, why he should not notice that she was very beautiful. But at that moment he is caught, and a kind of ratchet effect begins to operate: sin and crime follow sin and crime, and everyone is soon caught up in the snowball as it rushes downhill. And it is this point which Hebrew narrative makes supremely well through its economy and laconic, uncommented style, just as in another way Greek tragedy also makes it. For the reader, the tale serves as a warning, probably not against rape and murder, which few people ever commit, but certainly in favour of keeping up one's guard and paying attention to the danger that one's actions will have unforeseen and unintended consequences. That is why I said that the stories in the Hebrew Bible do not exactly teach duties or virtues, yet do engage us existentially and can deeply inform our moral life. If we want to know not what we must do and what we must avoid in order not actually to sin, but how to construct a moral world in which we can live as we should, such stories are the most powerful vehicles for conveying the risks which human beings run when they think their actions are morally neutral, and when they forget that everything they do is part of a web of cause and effect in which they are always inescapably enmeshed.

Like David, we find that there is no easy solution to

making the wrong decision. God can forgive sin, as he apparently forgives David's through the mouth of Nathan. But the consequences of the sin have a long afterlife, and the death of David and Bathsheba's child does not, in fact, lay the matter to rest. It rumbles on, much like the guilt in Aeschylus' *Oresteia*, but unlike that curse it is actually never purged by a divine intervention. The story seems to end with the confirmation of the kingdom in the hands of Solomon, Bathsheba's second child; yet even on his deathbed David is planting the seeds of further murders, by telling Solomon to take revenge on the enemies he had pardoned during his lifetime, and these are among Solomon's first acts as king (I Kings 2). There is an unremitting moral seriousness in this story, in which the possibly casual act of one hot afternoon has almost infinite consequences. One cannot really extract moral generalizations from these very particular events; yet they are a very powerful recommendation of living with integrity, and they make clear that the business of living well is no joke.

How does this discussion fit into a book about ethics in the Old Testament? If such a book were conceived as a statement of what the Old Testament regards as right and wrong, one could not make much more of the story of David than to list the crimes which it plainly regards as wrong, and pass on. My conviction, strengthened by Martha Nussbaum's insights into Greek tragedy and modern novels, is that any book on Old Testament ethics which would be obliged to relegate this story to a page while treating the laws in Leviticus, say, at great length, would inevitably be flawed, because it would not be doing justice to the particular genius of Hebrew literature but applying to it standards drawn from the quite different ethical world inhabited by modern or classical ethical theory. If we are to take stories like the story of David seriously as an ethical resource, then we shall have to understand the moral life as fed by reflection on the way narrators capture the essence of human persons in the way they tell their story, leading us to enter into the lives of those persons and understand what we share in common with them because we too are human. General moral principles are bound to operate in such stories, and they can be extracted and discussed. But the ethical interest of the stories does not lie there. It lies in the interplay of such principles with the flawed characters of the protagonists in the stories, producing complex actions in which we can recognize our own moral dilemmas and obligations.

3

Three Ethical Issues

So far I have tried to show how complex are the ethical ideas we can find in the Old Testament, but at the same time to indicate that there is some unity in its moral vision. One of the most striking features of the Old Testament is the way this ethical vision is expressed not only through laws and rules and precepts, but also – and perhaps primarily – through narratives or stories. The profundity of much that the Old Testament has to say in the field of ethics is bound up with the fact that it thus allows for the intricacy and untidiness of human life, and presents us with rounded personalities through whose interplay we can see ethical decision-making, and of course ethical failure, in action.

In this chapter I want to turn from these rather general points, and focus on a number of specific ethical issues, but always bearing in mind what we've established already, especially the need to look at narrative as well as law. I have chosen three issues which have a considerable contemporary relevance, yet where I believe the Old Testament has more to contribute to our debates than is generally thought. In each case I shall begin by returning to the argument of chapter 1, looking at the diversity but also the possible unity of the Old Testament witness; then I shall go on to examine some narrative texts and to ask how the theme of ethics and story can be brought to bear on the issue in question.

1. Ecology

Many, perhaps most, people who are actively 'green' regard the Judaeo-Christian tradition, and especially the Old Testament, as the source of many of the world's ecological ills. They point particularly to Genesis as having authorized human dominion over the natural world and encouraged the human race to exploit its resources for its own selfish ends. Gen. 1.28 reads, 'God blessed them, and God said to them, "Be fruitful and multiply, and fill the earth and subdue it; and have dominion over the fish of the sea and over the birds of the air and over every living thing that moves upon the earth."' What is worse, later in Genesis, after the flood, we read (Gen. 9.1), 'Be fruitful and multiply, and fill the earth. The fear of you and the dread of you shall be upon every beast of the earth, and upon every bird of the air, upon everything that creeps on the ground and all the fish of the sea; into your hand they are delivered. Every moving thing that lives shall be food for you.' This appears to justify the human exploitation of natural and animal resources, and to elevate human beings to a position of dominance in creation which rules out the sense of respect for the natural world that ecologists are so anxious to encourage.

In response to criticism of Judaism and Christianity along these lines it is perfectly reasonable to point to other texts that go in a different direction. Psalm 8, for example, picks up the language of Genesis and talks about all things being put under man's feet, but clearly thinks of this in terms of a sense of wonder and delight, and of humility that mere human beings have been deemed worthy to be enthroned like kings over the world God has made:

> When I look at thy heavens, the work of thy fingers,
>   the moon and the stars which thou hast established:
> what is man that thou art mindful of him,
>   and the son of man that thou dost care for him?
> Yet thou hast made him little less than God,
>   and dost crown him with glory and honour.
> Thou hast given him dominion over the works of thy
>   hands;
>   thou hast put all things under his feet (Ps. 8.3–6)

This may suggest that Christians are right to speak of the human relationship to the natural world in the Hebrew Bible in terms of stewardship, rather than domination in an oppressive sense. Soon after Gen. 1, after all, we see the first man in action, and he behaves as a gardener in Eden, living at peace with the animals and tending the garden. It is only after sin enters into this world and he is expelled from Eden that the ground begins to be recalcitrant, yielding thorns and thistles, pain establishes itself in the world, and animals become hostile and dangerous.

If we think of human beings in their stewardship of creation as kings and queens, it is worth reminding ourselves that the image of the good king in the Old Testament as in much other literature from the ancient world is a benign image. The good king guards and tends his people like a shepherd, he does not exploit and devour them. Hence to say that the created world is placed 'under his feet' does not necessarily have the oppressive overtones it appears to have in modern English. We might compare what is said about the seventh-century king of Judah, Jehoiakim, by Jeremiah, contrasting him with his father, Josiah:

Woe to him who builds his house by unrighteousness, and his upper rooms by injustice; who makes his neighbour serve him for nothing, and does not give him his wages; who says, 'I will build myself a great house with spacious upper rooms,' and cuts out windows for it, panelling it with cedar, and painting it with vermilion. Do you think you are a king because you compete in cedar? Did not your father eat and drink and do justice and righteousness? Then it was well with him. He judged the cause of the poor and needy; then it was well. Is not this to know me? says the LORD. But you have eyes and heart only for your dishonest gain, for shedding innocent blood, and for practising oppression and violence (Jer. 22.13–17).

If that is what being a good king amounts to, then the human race as rulers of creation are presumably not authorized to tear that creation apart, but should tend and care for it.

We can also point out that the negative side of this dominion, which puts animals and birds under the 'fear and dread' of their human masters, is clearly presented in

Genesis as the effect of sin. In Genesis 1 humans and animals alike are meant to be vegetarian (Gen. 1.29–30). Only after the Flood, when things return to the way they were but coarsened and sullied by human sin, is the slaughter of animals for food permitted, at the same time as the first legislation about murder is put in place. Violence is not part of the original intentions of the creator.

Thus we could whittle away at the case ecologists sometimes make against the Bible. We cannot deny that people have taken the texts in Genesis to authorize environmental exploitation, but we can argue that at least some of these texts did not originally have this implication; though if we are honest we are bound to confess that there is a residue of genuinely anti-ecological thinking within the biblical text.

But it may be useful to come at this topic from another angle. The real problem with a concern for the environment within Christian thinking is the extent to which Christians have always placed the emphasis on interpersonal ethics. Morality in Christianity is a matter of obligations, duties, and prohibitions about the way people interact with each other, whether as individuals or as corporate groups. In Christian ethics, as in most Western thinking about morality, moral imperatives apply to the way people behave to each other, within networks of commitment, obligation, hostility, and so on, and a person, a fellow moral agent, is the object of moral activity. There are no obligations towards sticks and stones. Animals are in a slightly ambivalent position, but on the whole are also not treated as part of the moral world. It is human beings that count.

Now ecological thinking seeks to overturn this fixation on persons, and urges that the physical world also has 'rights' which we may not ignore. In doing so it certainly runs counter to much traditional Christian teaching. Is it also opposed to the ideas of the Old Testament, taken in themselves? Perhaps not to quite the same extent. I remember my surprise when I first encountered the following text in Deuteronomy (20.19–20):

> When you besiege a city for a long time, making war against it in order to take it, you shall not destroy its trees by wielding an axe against them; for you may eat of them, but you shall not cut them down. Are the trees in the field men, that they should be besieged by you?

Later in the same section we come upon a law about the need to respect birds' nests (Deut. 22.6–7):

> If you chance to come upon a bird's nest, in any tree or on the ground, with young ones or eggs and the mother sitting upon the ground or upon the eggs, you shall not take the mother with the young.

These laws seem to presuppose some idea that human beings have obligations to the animal and vegetable world, that certain ways of acting towards them are 'unfair' or exploitative. The same kind of principle may lie behind the famous rule that 'you shall not boil a kid in its mother's milk' (Ex. 23.19). This is the origin of the distinctive Jewish custom of not mixing meat with milk, which is the determining factor in much Jewish cuisine and in the way Jewish kitchens are organized. No one knows quite what it originally meant, but it seems to rest on the same kind of principle as the law about birds' nests: that it is abhorrent to use the milk that would have fed the kid to cook it, a kind of perversion of nature, which does to an animal what anyone would regard as abominable if something analogous to it were done in the human world.

Once we allow examples like this, the whole world of Jewish food laws, which rests on chapters in Leviticus and Deuteronomy, suddenly begins to look as though it might be relevant. It has been usual for Christians to regard the laws of *kashrut*, the kosher system, as what is traditionally called 'ceremonial' law rather than as moral law – an interpretation which Jews dismiss with some exasperation, saying that Judaism is totally misunderstood if one tries to drive a wedge between what is moral and what is 'only' a matter of ritual observance. A well-lived Jewish life pays full attention to both, and does not in fact recognize a distinction between them. An ecological perspective might help us to see one reason among others why this might be so, even though it is not articulated in this way within Judaism. How human beings relate to animals, and to the world of food and drink, is not a matter of indifference from a moral point of view, but needs to take account of the relationship between the human realm and the animal and vegetable realm intended by the one who created them both. While the specifics of the food laws obviously cannot be derived from what the Bible says of this relationship, the fact that it gets encoded as it does in Judaism is not something that can be ignored as of no account. On the contrary, it takes seriously the ecology of human beings in the natural world in a way which deserves our admiration.

Another feature of Old Testament legislation that reflects an attitude of respect for the natural world is the institution of the sabbatical and jubilee years, when the land lies fallow (see Lev. 25). At one level we can say that the ancient Israelites had discovered the agricultural principle of fallow ground, as so many other cultures have done, and then dressed this up as a divine command. But it is quite clear that there is more to it than that, because the fallow year is consistently interpreted as something the land has a *right* to. In what Leviticus has to say about the exile of the sixth century, we find the idea that the people were removed from the land 'so that the land might enjoy its sabbaths' (Lev. 26.34–5), not in an agricultural but in a moral sense: the people's sins had put an intolerable strain on the land, from which it needed a fallow period to recover. The sabbatical years, like the weekly sabbath, represent a restoration of the land to an actually or symbolically unworked condition, in which it could be itself without human interference. These ideas seem to me potentially fruitful in the debate about ecology. I do not see them as resolving any specific difficulties, or providing the answer to any current dilemmas; I do think they confirm that ecology should be on the ethical agenda of anyone who claims to take the Bible seriously.

2. Sexual morality

In the area of ecology Christians probably do not think first of looking to the Old Testament. Where sexual morality is concerned, on the other hand, an appeal to the Bible is very common, and the Old Testament figures strongly in most people's perception of Christian moral norms. This is particularly clear in modern discussion of homosexuality, about which there are several Old Testament texts that seem quite unambiguously to forbid it, and is also true where questions of marriage and the family are concerned.

Because it is such a live issue today, I think it may be good to begin with the question of homosexuality – before broadening the discussion to look at the wider question of how the Old Testament can really guide us in the area of sexual morality.

It is well known that in several places the Old Testament laws forbid at least some homosexual practices: e.g. Lev. 20.13, 'If a man lies with a male as with a woman, both of them have committed an abomination; they shall be put to death'; cf. also Lev. 18.22, 'You shall not lie with a male as with a woman; it is an abomination.'

There are also two narrative texts in the Old Testament which deal with this theme, and which have traditionally been regarded as implying a great hostility to homosexuality, the conveniently numbered Gen. 19 and Judg. 19, two of what Phyllis Trible calls 'texts of terror', which seem to have some connection with each other.[1] Both of these are stories about the brutal rape of women, not of men: in Gen. 19 such rape is envisaged but prevented by divine intervention, in Judg. 19 it actually occurs, resulting in the death of the woman concerned, the concubine of a wandering Levite. But the point is that in both cases the threat to the woman arises because a group of men want to get their hands on *male* visitors to their city: in Genesis, on the two angels whom Lot has taken in, and in Judges on the Levite himself – 'Bring out the man who came into your house, that we may know him' (Judg. 19.22). The concubine's fate, and potentially though not actually the fate of Lot's young daughters, is to be as it were thrown to the wolves as a substitute for the men who, as honoured guests, must not be violated. 'No, my brethren, do not act so wickedly; seeing that this man has come into my house, do not do this vile thing. Behold, here are my virgin daughter and his concubine. Rape them and do with them what seems good to you; but against this man do not do so vile a thing' (Judg. 19.23–4).

It is not easy to get one's mind round these horrible stories, but this much can be said: the crime that is actually or potentially committed is clearly heterosexual rape, which is regarded as wrong in all the Israelite lawcodes as in most other documents from the ancient Near East. But the crime that is so brutally and unjustly prevented is a homosexual act, and thus it can be said that the stories only make sense on the supposition that homosexuality is wrong – that the author knew and approved the sort of provision we find in Leviticus. It is not by mistake that the sin of the city of Sodom, where in Gen. 19 this potential crime occurs, has traditionally been seen as homosexual in character – even though, incidentally, other biblical references to Sodom, such as those in Isa. 1.9–10, do not mention this.

Even here, though, things are more complicated than they look. Of course it is clear that the author does not approve of the men of Sodom, nor of the men of Gibeah in Judg. 19, but equally he does not approve of the Levite or of Lot for offering them a victim. It is plain that *within the story* all the men involved see the breach of hospitality involved in exposing a guest to ill-treatment as worse than the rape of wives and daughters, and it is only on the supposition that that is how the characters in the story see matters that the stories make sense. But it is not evident that the *narrator* sees things in that way: in the case of the Judges incident, it probably comes under the rubric 'In those days there was no king in Israel; every man did what was right in his own eyes' (Judg. 21.25). As so often in Hebrew narrative, no moral comment is passed, and we are left to make up our own minds. So far as homosexuality is concerned, what is being blamed here is clearly homosexual rape, not consensual relations. It seems to me very likely, in view of the passages in Leviticus, that the author would have regarded homosexual acts as wrong in all circumstances, but that cannot simply be deduced from these two stories, where a violent crime is envisaged. As is so often the case, narrative texts do not provide us with clear moral guidelines except in extreme cases: violent treatment of innocent victims is of course thoroughly wicked, but we knew that anyway. In the area where many modern people have uncertainties, the narrative does not really resolve matters. Instead it invites us to contemplate a terrible conjunction of wrong motives, evil actions, and uninformed consciences, leading to a human disaster. We are meant to disapprove of almost everything everyone in the story does, but it is hard to read off a 'moral' from it except at the most obvious level.

Similar things can be said of other narratives dealing with less extreme cases than the two 'texts of terror': marital and extramarital relations play a large part in the literature of ancient Israel, as they do in most literature everywhere in the world, but there is not much that can be turned into moral rules. Are we left, then, with simply the laws of the Pentateuch from which we have to generalize as best we can – the Ten Commandments, the laws in Leviticus and Deuteronomy, and perhaps the sayings of the prophets? I think this is unduly pessimistic. In the area of sexual morality there seems to be an underlying structure of assumptions and norms which inform narrative as well as law and prophecy, and by examining that it is possible at least to define the problem which the Old Testament poses for modern thinking about sexual conduct.

To judge from the evidence we have, the structures of family life changed comparatively little during the millennium covered by the Old Testament text. Polygamy, which is well attested in the pre-exilic period at least for kings and other upper-class people, seems more or less to have died out, and late books such as Tobit present us with a domestic picture of life in an extended family, but one based on monogamy. (The Old Testament nowhere condemns polygamy, however.) The person to whom the Ten Commandments are addressed is, as we saw, an adult male householder, under whose authority are a wife (only one, it seems to be implied), children, and aged parents who no longer have their own establishment but presumably live with their married son, together with slaves and livestock. This model is the foundation for everything the Old Testament has to say, explicitly or by implication, about human sexual conduct.

Sexual misconduct is defined as acts which breach the family structure implied in the Ten Commandments.

Adultery is sexual intercourse between a man and a married woman, in other words, it is defined asymmetrically. It is not adultery for a married man to have intercourse with an unmarried woman; if she is a virgin, he renders himself liable to having to marry her, as in many traditional societies, but if she is widowed or divorced no offence has been committed. Similarly, sexual relations with prostitutes are not adultery (and prostitution is nowhere forbidden in the Old Testament); nor is the use of concubines, that is, slaves who have an established position in the household and are a kind of half-wife. Adultery is intercourse with (and here ideas of possession come in) *another man's wife*. Old Testament legislation about sexual morality always has these overtones of being a kind of property law. It is not true to say that men in Israel were free to sleep with whomever they liked, because if they slept with a married woman then, at least according to the letter of the law, both partners faced the death penalty. But they were vastly freer than women, who had only one sexual option, namely their husbands, unless they were widowed or divorced.

The book of Proverbs, in its first nine chapters, provides some interesting light on adultery. The wisdom literature of Israel, and of other ancient Near Eastern nations, has a pronounced though limited streak of misogyny, and in Proverbs there are admonitions to the young man to whom it is supposedly addressed to avoid being ensnared by wicked women, who, it is implied, are always on the lookout for him (see Prov. 5 and 7). Some of these people are evidently foreign women – misogyny plus xenophobia is a potent brew – but some are definitely married Israelite

49

women who dress as prostitutes, precisely to give the impression that they are not married but sexually available. The result can be that our impressionable young man can be tricked into committing adultery, a capital crime: 'All at once he follows her, as an ox goes to the slaughter, or as a stag is caught fast till an arrow pierces its entrails; as a bird rushes into a snare, he does not know that it will cost him his life' (Prov. 7.22–23). The Old Testament entirely lacks a sense that sex is inherently sinful; but it does think it is dangerous. Only the institution of the family, as understood in that culture, keeps it under control.

It is in this context that extra-marital sexual activity is to be seen. Adultery is forbidden as an offence against the family and especially against its head, the adult male property-owner; it does not appear to be condemned for any harm it does emotionally, and in particular there is nowhere any consideration of the feelings of a wife as in any sense an offended party. Women in Old Testament law are certainly more than their husband's chattels – but then so are slaves, since they are given the right to marry and have their own, subordinate, family; but wives are just as certainly less than fully independent agents. All the legislation about sexual morality, and all the stories in which it is present, take this basic asymmetry for granted. It is not, I think, implied that either Lot or the Levite had the right to give daughters or concubines to the crowd clamouring at the door; but equally one cannot really imagine that the story could have continued 'but Lot's daughters refused'. They are under their father's authority until they come under their husband's. All this would have been entirely familiar in Western society one hundred years ago, and it is still familiar today across the greater part of the world. It is hard to see how the Old Testament could have worked with other presuppositions without falling entirely out of its setting.

It is clear, at the same time, that women in Israelite society in many periods had a high degree of freedom in daily activity, and one way in which the Old Testament is unusual is in the number of strong female characters its stories contain: one thinks of Deborah (Judg. 4–5), Abigail (I Sam. 25), Jezebel (I Kings 19 and 21; II Kings 9) or Esther. But there can't be much doubt that they exist in a society which is what is now usually called 'patriarchal'.

Adultery is seen as a breach in the stability of society, then, as prostitution and what Christians have traditionally called fornication are not. When we come to homosexual acts, however, we seem from the OT's perspective to be moving on to stranger ground. The immediate context of the laws against homosexual acts is a list of sexual activities that are regarded not just as breaking good order, but as unnatural or 'abominable' – ideas I shall be discussing in the next chapter. Homosexual activity is classed with bestiality, incest, and other taboo acts, for which the reader is expected to feel a kind of automatic revulsion. Many people certainly did, and just as certainly still do. At one level, then, there is no doubt that the Old Testament is 'against' homosexual acts, though it never defines exactly what acts these are. But there is one feature of the Old Testament which is not often noticed, and which even if we share its feeling of revulsion should make us pause and take stock.

The stories in Gen. 19 and Judg. 19 make sense only on the assumption that sexual desire is largely indiscriminate. To persuade the crowd baying at the door to abandon its pursuit of a male guest, a female victim is provided. In modern terms I suppose one could say that the men of Sodom or of Gibeah are assumed to be bisexual, but this gives quite the wrong impression. The storyteller thinks of them simply as in the grip of sexual lust, a lust so intense that any sexual object will do. The idea of sexual *orientation* seems to be entirely lacking. A fashionable way of thinking about homosexuality in the Church of England today is to distinguish sharply between sexual orientation and sexual activity, and to say that sexual orientation is ethically neutral; it is only about homosexual acts that there needs to be ethical discussion. If I say that this distinction is not 'scriptural', I don't say so in order to condemn homosexuality: I am concerned at the moment with describing what is in the Old Testament, not with defending it. What is unscriptural about the distinction is simply that, so far as I can see, the notion of sexual orientation is wholly lacking from the Bible anyway. *Anyone* might be tempted to commit adultery, bestiality, or incest, or to engage in homosexual activity: sexual desire is a random force, not contained within some prearranged format. There is no such condition, in the Old Testament's perspective, as 'being homosexual' or 'being heterosexual': human beings are simply 'sexual', and there is a wide range of things they may choose to do with their sexuality, many of them forbidden.

As with so many of the issues we have examined, this means that the Old Testament is even stranger to us than we may expect. It is equally difficult to accept it or to reject it, because it does not seem designed to deal with our particular problems. It is the answer to questions not identical with those we are asking, within a society which is not ours. If, for example, we are to accept its judgment on homosexuality, we must be aware that this made sense against a social background in which the extended family was seen as the main legitimate outlet for sexual desire, but alongside perfectly legal prostitution and the existence of concubines. Taking one element out of the overall system of sexual morality may be to distort what the Old Testament is saying. On the other hand, there might be elements in the Old Testament's moral system which rest on an appeal to what is obviously good at all times and in all places, to what is 'natural' and not 'abominable'; and we may think that some sexual activity falls under that heading. I shall be looking in the next chapter at the possibility that some of the Old Testament's moral teaching rests on what may be called a 'natural law' approach. One important question in the study of Old Testament ethics is which areas of sexual morality belong to which category, for the authors of the Old Testament themselves. The question for the ethicist is then what to do about this finding.

3. Property

The modern Christian, faced with the question of what the Old Testament says about property, is likely to return to an idea discussed above, the idea of *stewardship*. Certainly when the use of money, time, and talent comes up, as in connection with church stewardship schemes, it tends to be emphasized that according to the Bible there is no absolute property: what we say we 'own' is held in trust from God, and we are stewards, not really owners. This is indeed one important aspect of biblical thought about the ownership of property. Deuteronomy, for example, continually stresses that Yahweh gives his people the land, but that it continues to belong to him: Israel has no rights in the land, but possesses it by divine permission (see Deut. 26). Compare Ps. 44.3: 'not by their own sword did they win the land, nor did their own arm give them victory; but thy right hand, and thy arm, and the light of thy countenance'. As in the Epistle to the Hebrews, the Israelites are regarded as living in the land on a kind of permanently temporary basis; it is a sort of permanent loan to them, never in an absolute sense their own (cf. Heb. 11.8–10).

However, I become rather doubtful about the idea of stewardship in the Old Testament, when it is applied to individual property rights. So far as I can see, there is nothing to suggest that *individuals* were regarded as holding their land on loan from God. What was central was the idea of *ancestral* land, the land that one's family had always possessed, which was seen (in a rather legendary way) as having been assigned by lot to each family at the time when the land was first settled, after the conquest by Joshua. This land was seen as inalienable. The classic place where this notion is elaborated is in I Kings 21, the story of Naboth's vineyard. King Ahab, who ruled the northern kingdom of Israel in the ninth century, wants to get his hands on a piece of land belonging to a certain Naboth, which adjoins his own royal property; but Naboth refuses to let him have it. To get it, Ahab (on the advice of Jezebel) resorts to a ruse: he gets Naboth accused of having slandered himself, the king, and also of having blasphemed, both capital offences. Then, when Naboth has been executed, his land comes to the king automatically instead of passing to Naboth's descendants (we do not know of this principle from anywhere else, but the story only makes sense if this is so). What is striking and important about the story from the point of view of property-law is that Ahab's original approach to Naboth does not imply that he has any claim to the land as king, and nor is it a threat to take it from Naboth by force: he says, 'Give me your vineyard . . . and I will give you a better vineyard for it; or, if it seems good to you, I will give you its value in money' (I Kings 21.2) – not at all an unreasonable suggestion, as we should think. But Naboth's reaction is furious: 'The LORD forbid that I should give you the inheritance of my fathers' (I Kings 21.3). Land is not seen as something one can freely dispose of, and therefore is also not something one can buy: it descends from the past as an inalienable possession.

This attitude to one's land is common to a great many traditional societies, and is far from dead in the modern world. It underlies much of what the prophets have to say about those who dispossess others of their land. Isaiah, for example, says: 'Woe to those who join house to house, who add field to field, until there is no more room, and you are made to dwell alone in the midst of the land' (Isa. 5.8). This presumably implies that people were doing just what Ahab had intended, adding other people's property to their own to make larger and larger estates. It is not said, and probably not implied, that they were *stealing* this land; however they were acquiring it, the building up of great estates was a sin in itself. Isaiah seems to have believed that everyone ought to live on a smallholding, avoiding the inequalities of landowners and serfs. The same is probably true of Micah: 'They covet fields, and seize them; and houses, and take them away' (Micah 2.2); and the divine punishment for this will be in kind: 'Among our captors he divides our fields', just as Isaiah sees it as consisting in the coming desolation of these artificial great estates: 'Surely many houses shall be desolate, large and beautiful houses, without inhabitant' (Isa. 5.9).

I've already mentioned the sabbatical and jubilee years, and the latter has a particular concern for the preservation of property rights. It comes from a period when it is established that land can be bought and sold – a period, therefore, presumably later than Isaiah and Micah – but it legislates against any permanent alienation of ancestral property. Lev. 25.13–16 reads: 'In this year of jubilee each of you shall return to his own property. And if you sell to your neighbour or buy from your neighbour, you shall not wrong one another. According to the number of years after the jubilee, you shall buy from your neighbour, and according to the number of years for crops he shall sell to you. If the years are many you shall increase the price, and if the years are few you shall diminish the price.' In other words, property can be sold only on a leasehold arrangement, and reverts to the freeholder at the jubilee. Whether this was ever carried out in practice we don't know, and the jubilee year system may be entirely wishful thinking anyway; but undoubtedly it reflects a distinctive attitude towards ancestral land.

So far as property other than real-estate is concerned, the Old Testament does not seem to have much to say that is distinctive. It has no reflections on people's stewardship of their ordinary property, and it assumes that things may be bought and sold provided this is at a fair price (there are many injunctions against having different scales for buying and selling: see Lev. 19.35–36; Deut. 25.13–16; Prov. 11.1, 20.23). Nor is there any ideal of 'holy poverty' in the Old Testament, so far as I can see. Those who are poor may be regarded as also innocent and hence the object of God's compassion, if they are poor because others have stolen from them or oppressed them, but certainly not if they are poor because they are lazy, as the book of Proverbs continually points out (see Prov. 6.6–11, 24.30–34). The ethos of the Old Testament is in this respect what might now be seen as right-wing: it is scandalous to make others poor unjustly, and the person who does so deserves punishment; but it is also scandalous to make oneself poor by idleness, and those who do deserve all they get. I cannot see that the Old Testament moves on to any higher level of sophistication than this. Its socio-economic analysis is fairly basic, and the complexities of a developed commercial society are beyond its grasp, as we would expect from such a document.

4

Divine Commands or
Natural Law?

In the previous chapters I have concentrated mostly on the
content of ethics in the Old Testament – what courses of
conduct are judged good or bad – and on how this
information is conveyed, whether through laws or through
narratives. But much ethical enquiry, especially in the
realm of moral philosophy, is concerned more with the
basis of ethics: how it comes about that this or that type of
action is right or wrong, or indeed why it is that there are
any moral obligations at all. Within the area of Christian
discussion of morality, there are (to put it very crudely)
two major traditions of theological ethics. One of them
sees human moral obligation as deriving from the express
commands of God, as a matter of what is technically called
'positive' law: acts are good or bad according to whether
God has commanded or forbidden them. The other sees
the source of ethics as the natural law, an ethical system
inherent in the way things are – a kind of innate moral
force in the world. This derives from God as creator of the
natural order, rather than by way of positive commandments.

Divine Commands or Natural Law?

Within the Christian churches this distinction has commonly been correlated with different attitudes towards the Bible. People who think the Bible to be central and indeed primary within the life of the church, which until the Second Vatican Council meant in effect Protestants, are likely to look askance at the natural law tradition of moral philosophy as in effect somewhat deistic. They see it as pushing God off into a realm where he may be the remote origin of moral obligation, but is not present in his creation as the one who teaches human beings how they should live. It overlooks, such people would say, the fact that God has actually spoken to men and women through the scriptures, not leaving them to deduce from the observation of some kind of natural order how they ought to behave, but giving them explicit directives. In the twentieth century Karl Barth was particularly active in insisting that God rules the world (and the church, and the individual) by positive law, of which the Ten Commandments are the most obvious example. The good for humanity is what God decrees it to be, not what human beings can deduce. Barth's opposition to any kind of natural law is simply an application, within the ethical sphere, of his opposition to natural theology.[1] God is the Divine Commander, and his voice is to be obeyed. This understanding of the matter is linked very strongly to an attachment to the Bible as the source of ethical teaching. If the Bible is to be central, then (Barth believed) positive law will be the obvious model for understanding ethics, since the Bible consists of, or at least contains, representations of divine speech concerning morality, presented as directives from God to the human race, or at least to Israel and the church.

Conversely, natural law traditions have tended to flourish where a perception of biblical authority has been weaker. Until the Second Vatican Council Roman Catholic teaching on ethics scarcely mentioned biblical texts, but worked philosophically and from first principles, asking what is or is not compatible with human nature as analysed philosophically. This is one reason why Catholic moral theology has felt free to issue rulings about the right way to live for all men and women, while Protestant moral teaching has often concerned itself only with the right way of life for those who have made a decision for God in Christ and therefore live within the fellowship of the church. Catholic moral teaching has had the strength of its more universal claim, based on a natural law analysis. But it has found it hard to relate to the Bible; and now that biblical texts are much more central in Catholicism, there is sometimes a difficulty in knowing what to do with them, how to graft them on to a moral tradition whose starting-point really lies elsewhere. The Bible as positive law disrupts that Catholic system. William Spohn, in his *What are they saying about Scripture and Ethics?*,[2] devised the excellent shorthand phrase 'Scripture as moral reminder' to encapsulate the place of the Bible in traditional Catholic teaching. What is right or wrong is known by the church as a deduction from natural law. Scripture comes in, not to legislate, but to illustrate: to show us, by examples and exhortations, what obedience to the natural law looks like in practice. It exists to remind us of what we already know.

I have set out traditional Protestant and Catholic positions in this very simplified form not in order to judge between them, but to emphasize an assumption that they have in common. This is the assumption that ethics in the Bible is a matter of positive rather than of natural law. For a Protestant such as Barth, natural law cannot be the essence of ethics because God's freely uttered word, embodied in scripture, is the positive law which governs Christian conduct. For traditional Catholics, the Bible cannot be central because it contains only positive law, and natural law has to have the pre-eminence. Disagreement between Catholics and Protestants rest on a prior agreement to the effect that the Bible corresponds to positive, not natural law.

In this chapter I want to question this consensus, and to suggest that natural law occurs within the Bible as well as outside it. The biblical writers often argue not from what God has declared or revealed, but from what is apparent on the basis of the nature of human life in society. Thus the simple contrast between natural law and biblical revelation will not do; whatever account we give of the place of the Bible in moral theology, it will have to be more complicated than that.

To come at the matter gradually, we may begin by noticing some places in the Old Testament where moral obligation seems to be regarded as a matter of human moral consensus, not necessarily resting on a theological basis at all. The clearest case of this is to be found in the oracles in Amos 1.3–2.3. Here the prophet denounces a number of atrocities or war-crimes committed by various nations surrounding Israel: the Arameans of Damascus, the Philistines, the Moabites, the Ammonites. None of the offences they are said to have committed is mentioned in

Old Testament law, and in any case, of course, Old Testament law does not legislate for the conduct of foreigners but only of Israelites. The logic of the prophet's attack seems to be that all these nations knew or ought to have known that certain practices in time of war, such as enslaving whole populations or torturing conquered enemies, are unacceptable. We know that he was correct in this assumption.[3] Most ancient Near Eastern nations had well developed codes of practice about what might or might not legitimately be done during a military campaign – codes which, needless to say, they often broke, as nations at war have always done, but which enabled them at least to complain of the conduct of their enemies. What is striking about Amos' denunciations is that for the most part the crimes in question do not seem to have been committed against Israel – so there is no element of national self-interest about it. He simply assumes that other nations have a moral conscience, and that atrocities are wrong and are known to be wrong by whomever and against whomever they are committed.

The term 'natural law' would be overstated as a way of describing ideas like these. Amos does not say that the concept of war-crimes rests on an analysis of the orders of nature, only that it is one everyone shares. He does not even say that God lies behind the concept, though he certainly thinks God avenges breaches of the code, since each oracle concludes by saying that God will send a fire on the capital city of the offending nation, either through natural disaster or by military conquest. Nevertheless we certainly have a phenomenon here that cannot be described in terms of divine positive law. It is neither said nor implied that

God has communicated with these foreign nations, still less that he has expressly forbidden them to commit atrocities; it is simply assumed that they know such acts to be wrong.

We move closer to what Christian moral thinking has understood by natural law when we turn from Amos to his younger contemporary, Isaiah. Isaiah reserves his most critical comments not so much for offences against the law – though certainly there is plenty about bribery and corruption, misappropriation of property, and injustice (Isa. 1.23; 3.9; 5.8–9, 23; 10.1–2) – but for ways of acting which breach a kind of natural order in things. Pride seems to be his primary target, whether this means a delight in personal appearance (as in his rather misogynist attacks on the upper-class women of Jerusalem in 3.16–4.1), the self-aggrandizement of the royal Secretary of State Shebna, who is building himself an expensive family tomb in Jerusalem in spite of having no family connections there (22.15–19), or the pride of the Judaean kings who put their trust in their armies and the defences they have built instead of in Yahweh, the God of Israel (31.1–2). A great variety of what Isaiah sees as moral failings are thus brought under the rubric of pride. If we ask what is wrong with being proud, the answer seems to be that it represents a human attempt to be like God – something like the sin of Adam and Eve in Gen. 3. And this in turn is wrong, not because God has forbidden it, but because it misunderstands the essentially lowly place of human beings in the world order. It represents a self–assertion which wants to overturn the proper order of things for selfish motives. The sin of Israel, like the sin of the king of Assyria, can be summed up in these words: 'Shall the axe vaunt itself over him who hews with it, or the saw magnify itself against him who wields it? As if a rod should wield him who lifts it, or as if a staff should lift him who is not wood!' (Isa. 10.15). It is an overturning of what Shakespeare called 'degree', the proper hierarchical ordering of the universe:

> Take but degree away, untune that string,
> And hark what discord follows. Each thing meets
> In mere oppugnancy. The bounded waters
> Should lift their bosoms higher than the shores
> And make a sop of all this solid globe;
> Strength should be lord of imbecility,
> And the rude son should strike his father dead.
> Force should be right – or rather, right and wrong,
> Between whose endless jar justice resides,
> Should lose their names, and so should justice too.
> Then everything includes itself in power,
> Power into will, will into appetite;
> And appetite, an universal wolf,
> So doubly seconded with will and power,
> Must make perforce an universal prey,
> And last eat up himself
> (*Troilus and Cressida*, Act 1, Scene 3).

Isaiah has a series of 'woe' oracles against various offenders which uses the same conceptuality: 'Woe to those who call evil good and good evil, who put darkness for light and light for darkness, who put bitter for sweet and sweet for bitter! Woe to those who are wise in their own eyes, and shrewd in their own sight!' (Isa. 5.20–21).

As he says in 29.16, 'You turn things upside down!' (just one word in Hebrew, 'your turning').

The whole way of thinking that holds together all Isaiah's comments on the moral conduct of his contemporaries has more in common with a natural law theory of ethics than with a system of positive or revealed law. Some of what Isaiah finds to condemn is also condemned in the legal codes of the Old Testament: examples would be perversion of the course of justice, oppression of the poor, and the taking of bribes (cf. Ex. 23.1–3, 6–8). Other sins could be the subject of laws but in fact are not: for example, drunkenness and excessive feasting, which the prophets in general criticize (see Isa. 5.22), but which are nowhere forbidden in the law. But such attitudes as pride and arrogance, and a failure to recognize the majesty of God through inappropriately self-assertive behaviour, hardly fall within the scope of what laws, in the literal sense, could even theoretically cover. And there is no reason to think that people in Israel believed God to have pronounced on such matters. Nor does Isaiah say that he has done so: he simply appeals to a moral sense in his hearers which will see that a refusal to accept the moral orders of the world is wicked.

Since prophecy is perhaps most people's paradigm case for revealed or positive divine law, this conclusion may be surprising. One of the major prophets of the Old Testament turns out to be close to having a natural law theory of ethics. But this is less curious when we take into account a fact about Isaiah which has long been generally accepted among Old Testament scholars, namely his closeness to what is called the 'wisdom tradition', the tradition of aphoristic teaching best represented in the Old Testament by the book of Proverbs. In Proverbs there is scarcely any use of the picture of God as lawgiver or commander. Where God does appear, it is as the one who watches over the operations of moral order in the world and avenges wrongdoing, but scarcely ever as the origina-tor of particular moral imperatives. This is not at all to say that the wisdom tradition is 'secular' in character, in the sense that God is absent from it; rather, the *mode* of his presence is different from that in the laws or, indeed, in many of the narrative books of the Old Testament. There God intervenes in the world, tells people to do this or that, and has to be obeyed as the supreme legislator. In the wisdom literature, on the other hand, God is a more back-ground presence.

For the wisdom writers – not only in Israel but through-out most of the ancient Near East – the role of God (or the gods, or 'the divine') is primarily to watch over a kind of abstract concept called in Israel 'justice' or 'righteousness' and in other cultures personified as a semi-divine being: 'ma'at' in Egypt, for example. This 'cosmic order', as it is sometimes called, is the principle that holds the universe together – at the physical level, a kind of cosmic glue – and around which human moral life has to be organized. 'Wisdom' is essentially the ability to live one's life in accordance with such order, at both the physical and the moral level: to be skilful in one's occupation, sensible and sagacious in one's decisions, and moral in one's whole way of life. Obedience to divine commands is at best only one small aspect of the whole system, and indeed where divine commands do appear they tend to be seen as specifications of how cosmic order should be maintained in a particular sphere of activity, rather than as a kind of overarching principle. What the Old Testament sums up as 'righteousness', *tsedeq*, is the whole way of living which someone who has an eye to cosmic order will follow, rather than a particular ordinance laid down by God.

The wisdom literature used to be regarded as marginal in biblical study, and if Barth was able to treat positive divine law as the only model within the Old Testament, that is because when he was writing biblical scholars themselves took little interest in the wisdom tradition, which they saw as a rather foreign body within Old Testament literature. In recent years, and especially under the influence of another Swiss scholar, Hans Heinrich Schmid, we have started to see this downgrading of wisdom and its preoccupations as something of an aberration in twentieth-century Old Testament studies.[4] For Schmid, the primary horizon of the Old Testament is not God's choice of Israel and the giving to them of the law, but the creation of the world and the moral order that derives from its created character. This implies that morality is first and foremost a matter of human beings recognizing their finite, created status and seeking a way of life which embodies their sense of belonging in the hierarchical universe whose head and origin is God. In other words, the underlying moral system of the Old Testament, on which the tradition of positive law has been superimposed, is more or less the system espoused by Isaiah, and worked out in detail in wisdom writings such as Proverbs. This neatly inverts the usual assumption that the Bible is all about God uttering imperatives to his chosen people, and reinstates instead a concern with the natural moral order of the created world which is not so far from a traditional Catholic concern for natural law (Schmid, by the way, is a Calvinist).

From this perspective natural law begins to look more common in the Old Testament than most people think – indeed, there's a risk that we shall start to find it everywhere. Even some of what are presented in the biblical text itself as positive laws may begin to look like expressions of a concern for natural order. The extreme case might be the food laws, in Lev. 11 and Deut. 14, the biblical basis for the complex system of dietary rules that is one of the most obviously distinctive features of modern Judaism, especially in its orthodox form. If ever there was a case of positive law, whose validity depends entirely on the will of the lawgiver and not at all on any inherent rightness in the law's content, this, we may feel, is it. Why is it permissible to eat sparrows but not seagulls, sheep but not camels, cod but not prawns? Surely only because God has commanded it, quite inscrutably, and we have to do what God tells us. There is a story in a rabbinic source (Numbers Rabbah 19) about a similarly incomprehensible piece of legislation, the law in Num. 19.1–9 about the use of the blood and ashes of a red heifer in ritual atonement for sin. A Gentile asked the famous rabbi Johanan ben Zakkai the reason for this law, and he produced all kinds of rational explanations; but after the Gentile had gone, his disciples asked him for the true reason, and he said simply, '"I have ordered an ordinance and decreed a decree, and no mortal must transgress my decree", as it is written (Num. 19.2), "This is the ordinance of the Torah".' Rationalizing explanations were for Gentiles; for Israelites, an awareness that God is the lawgiver should suffice. It is hard to see how one could have a more positive law than this, or be farther removed from any idea of natural law.

Yet here too matters are more complicated than they seem. The very chapters of the Pentateuch that contain the food laws also contain an explanation or rationale for at least some of them. Land animals are 'clean', that is, permitted as food, if they have cloven hoofs and also chew the cud, otherwise not: hence camels are unclean because they are cud-chewing or ruminant but not cloven-hoofed, and pigs are unclean because they are cloven-hoofed but not ruminant. To us the 'because' here is exceedingly mysterious, but it is produced in the text of Leviticus as though it makes the matter obvious. This means one of two things. Either the author is simply rationalizing after the event, i.e. he has a list of clean and unclean animals and has hit, fortuitously, on a principle that would generate it, even though in reality the origin of the list is quite different, perhaps entirely non-rational; or else within his culture there was indeed something obvious about the principle.

Until comparatively recently most commentators probably preferred the first explanation. They said, for example, that the 'real' reason why certain animals were deemed unclean was that they were offered in sacrifice in neighbouring cultures and therefore were taboo for the Israelites; or that people in Israel had discovered how dangerous it is to eat pigs or shellfish in a hot climate and had given this a divine sanction by inventing the category of 'unclean' animals. A new explanation was introduced into this discussion by the social anthropologist Mary Douglas in her now famous book *Purity and Danger*.[5]

Douglas argued that the reasons given for the cleanness and uncleanness of certain animals were the real reasons, that is, that people really did think there was something wrong with non-ruminant ungulates and non-ungulate ruminants, that such animals were somehow defective or unsatisfactory, and this meant they should not form part of the human diet. She explained this by postulating a notion of the natural and the unnatural, in which anything that crosses what are perceived as the natural boundaries between classes of things is felt to be unsatisfactory, defective, and even dangerous. She noted that there are other laws in the Old Testament that seem to operate with this distinction, for example the laws against wearing a garment made with two different kinds of fabric, sowing a field with two different sorts of seed (Deut. 22.9–11, cf. Lev. 19.19), and for that matter committing incest, where the distinction between what is sexually available (members of another family) and what is sexually unavailable (members of one's own family) is eroded (Lev. 18.6–18). This last example is one of the few remaining taboos in Western society, and if we consider how we react towards it we can perhaps begin to imagine how it would feel to perceive certain animals too as 'unnatural'. In the ancient world sphinxes terrified people because they were mixtures, animals from a nightmare, and the beasts in Daniel 7 are surely frightening chiefly because it's impossible to say what they are: they are made up of bits of everything.

Now of course the question remains why anyone should have thought that chewing the cud ought to go with having cloven hoofs, and that there was something wrong with an animal that didn't conform to this pattern, and Mary Douglas gets us no nearer to answering that question. But her hypothesis remains a powerful one, because it avoids our having to say, like the rabbi in the story, that the reason for the prohibition of certain animals was rooted in an entirely non-rational divine decree. It may not look rational to us, but it was probably perceived as rational in ancient Israel, at least in some (probably rather remote) period. And this immediately brings it into contact with the question of natural law. Just as a modern Catholic ethicist may condemn abortion, say, by arguing that it does not do justice to the nature of human persons, so in ancient Israel people may have thought that certain animals were an aberration which failed to conform to what was natural to animals. It is almost impossible to convey what was meant in modern English without the words 'nature' and 'natural' coming in somewhere, even though biblical Hebrew had no terms corresponding to these. The rationale of the food laws seems to be something close to an idea of 'natural law', radically different from what we might mean by that in many ways, but at the same time close enough to justify the use of the term, even if in inverted commas.

My suggestion therefore is that there is a great deal of natural law in the Old Testament, and that something like this is the basis for ethics not only in rather sophisticated thinkers such as the prophets, but also at an underlying level in texts which go back to a pre-intellectual stage. At many periods and in many different social strata people in ancient Israel perceived moral obligation as having to do with cosmic order, with how the world was to be understood and classified. So far from positive law being the only approach to ethics in the Old Testament, natural law is much more pervasive and persistent.

At the same time we must not underestimate the extent to which Israelites also believed that God had issued positive decrees which they had to obey, whether or not they could be traced back to some supposed natural order in the world. Positive law appears at two levels: first, in specific commandments which God is said to have uttered, and secondly, as the overarching framework within which, over the course of time, people in Israel came to understand morality.

Examples of specific divine commandments are easy to find in the Old Testament, and it is because they are so plentiful that people came to deny the possibility of any other kind of basis for morality in the first place. We have already discussed the Ten Commandments, but the Pentateuch is full of other divine commands which the people are to obey simply because they are given by God. Deuteronomy in particular abounds in imperatives, instructing the people what they are to do on the basis that it is God who commands it. The positive basis of ethical obligation is seen especially where the covenant between Yahweh and Israel is in view, for the covenant is essentially a contract, in which the terms whose observance will constitute performance of the contract are specified for the benefit of both parties (see Deut. 8, 28, 30). To live within the covenant involves binding oneself to do the things that the covenant partner, Yahweh, requires, and his requirements do not have to be justified in terms of any inherent correctness: they are binding because they are his requirements. At the same time, Deuteronomy does recommend Yahweh's laws as very good laws: 'What great nation is there, that has statutes and ordinances so righteous as all this law which I set before you this day?' (4.8). This implies some standard by which Yahweh's laws can be measured, which must logically be prior to those laws, and this probably lands us back in natural law again. Nevertheless in general the impression given is that the laws are binding because of who gave them, rather than for their inherent merit. Obedience to them is a test of loyalty to Yahweh, the God of Israel.

In the prophets, too, Israel is condemned as disobedient to its God. We find this idea at the beginning of the book of Isaiah, despite the strong appeal to natural law also in that book. 'The ox knows its owner, and the ass its master's crib; but Israel does not know, my people does not consider' (Isa. 1.3). The loyalty and obedience of dumb animals are superior to anything Israel can demonstrate. In another image, the prophet pictures Israel as a slave, severely beaten yet still unwilling to stop 'rebelling' (1.5–6). In other prophets the theme of disobedience is even clearer than in Isaiah, with Hosea comparing the relationship between Yahweh and Israel to a marriage (Hos. 1–3). Much is often made of this as an image of great tenderness, but even if that theme is present, more obvious is the implication that Israel, like a loyal wife, owes her divine husband obedience. The marriage relationship in Israel was highly asymmetrical, and wives were primarily a central part of their husband's household, owing him obedience just as did his children and his slaves. In chapter 2 Israel as Yahweh's unfaithful wife is to be disciplined, just as Hosea says he 'disciplined' his own wife, until she learns to obey her master, that is, to do the things he tells her to do with the right attaching to his superior status. The passages surveyed in this paragraph are a long way from attitudes to human relationships that most people now would find acceptable.

Thus there are many specific examples of human morality as obedience to positive divine law. But at least in its present form the Old Testament also sees positive law as the model for the whole of the morality that derives from God: in other words, even the elements of natural law that we have been able to find are included, for the final editors of the Old Testament, under the rubric of obedience to God – and this, indeed, is why most readers of the Bible take it for granted that obedience to positive divine law is the only model that scripture provides. The food laws, for example, as they now appear in Leviticus and Deuteronomy are set in the context of God's speech to Moses or Moses' speech to Israel: they are what God tells the people they must do. Prophetic comments on the morality of the nation are treated as having an implied 'Thus says the LORD' in front of them – even though as a matter of fact it is only with predictions of future events, never with the moral analysis of why these events will be as they will, that the formula 'Thus says the LORD' occurs. Thus even those moral utterances that were originally an expression of conventional or natural morality tend to be contextualized so as to make them instances of positive law, of 'revelation' if you like, in which God is giving directives that derive wholly from his will and do not rest on natural human intuitions about ethics.

Once the Old Testament came to form a fixed canon for both Jews and Christians there was a natural enough tendency to read everything in it as revelation. This had a most radical effect on the wisdom literature. Proverbs which were originally a distillation of human wisdom come to be read as the expression of divine advice or legislation. Thus in the Mishnah – an authoritative collection of rabbinic rulings about legal matters compiled in the second century AD – the book of Proverbs is one of the most quoted texts from the whole Hebrew scriptures as a source for revealing the divine will. In the apocryphal book called Ecclesiasticus, or the Wisdom of Jesus son of Sira, the 'wisdom' which in earlier texts of the wisdom tradition had been human wisdom is turned into divine wisdom and identified with the Torah, the Jewish blueprint for how to live that is the concrete expression of God's revelation of his positive law. The whole of scripture, seen in this way, is God telling us what we must do, and any sense that it might contain some natural human morality or natural law is squeezed out. Divine commandments can be extracted from Proverbs just as much as from Leviticus or Deuteronomy; indeed, they can also be extracted from narrative material, by treating the characters in Old Testament stories as examples of good or bad conduct. In fact, as we have seen, Old Testament narratives are often not at all well adapted to this treatment. The moral world the characters inhabit is frequently much more complicated than an assessment based on answering the simple 'yes or no?' question of whether they obeyed the law. And the characters in these stories themselves seem to appeal to standards of morality that are not connected to divine ordinances. For example, when in the story of David's children Tamar is about to be raped by her brother Amnon she says, 'Such a thing is not done in Israel; do not do this wanton folly' (II Sam. 13.12) – using the language of custom and convention rather than speaking in terms of divine revelation. But a theological reading of this story such as appealed to Jews or Christians at the beginning of our era tended to assume that Amnon's sin was disobedience to the law, and that therefore must have been what Tamar meant.

When a theologian such as Karl Barth declares that all morality in the Old Testament is obedience to the divine Commander, he is not therefore necessarily mistaken, for the Bible in its finished or 'canonical' form has been so construed by Christians and Jews for many centuries, and it can be so read. In this chapter I have tried to show that, underlying the present form of the text, we can discern earlier stages in which morality was conceived in a much more diverse way, with the model 'obedience to God's positive laws' as only one option. If we wish, we can insist on remaining with the final level of the text's meaning, with the Bible as Jews and Christians have received and traditionally interpreted it. But I think we can also be permitted to dig beneath the surface, and to show that in these ancient documents there are, even if in a rudimentary form, approaches to ethics which see it as resting on a foundation more like what Western tradition has called 'natural law' than most readers of the Bible ever suspect.

5

Why Should we be Moral?

In the last chapter I argued that something we could call 'natural law' has a much more prominent place in the Old Testament than is usually thought. One aspect of this is that the writers of the Old Testament – or the speakers, such as the prophets, who lie behind them – often appealed to a kind of shared moral sense which they thought everyone had in common. What they had to tell people about morality was not that God had, inscrutably, commanded this or forbidden that, but that the basic principles of ethical obligation were accessible to all irre-spective of any special divine revelation. Consequently no one could claim immunity from divine punishment on the grounds that they did not know what they were doing was wrong. This is certainly the line of argument in Amos 1.3–2.3.

There is a further way in which Old Testament writers argue or reason with their readers, and this is by adding what are technically called 'motive clauses' to their appeals for people to act more morally. Morality is not only *grounded* – in the will of God or in the natural law – but also *motivated*. This can be seen as early as what is uni-versally recognized as the oldest Israelite law code, the so-called 'Book of the Covenant' in Ex. 21–24 – usually referred to in Jewish scholarship as the *mishpatim* or judgments. The Book of the Covenant is purportedly the detailed commandments Moses was given for Israel immediately after the Ten Commandments had been revealed. It is indeed possible to see it as a detailed spelling out of the implications of the Commandments, though it doesn't follow them at all closely in order. Most scholars think this was the law code by which Israel lived throughout much of the pre-exilic period, say from the time of the judges (eleventh century BC?) down to the reign of Josiah in the seventh century, who substituted for it the law code that forms the central section of Deuteronomy (roughly 12–26). (This for the most part is an updated and expanded version of the Book of the Covenant.) But even the present text of the Book of the Covenant is probably an expanded version of the original legal code, for as it stands it contains material that is not in any straightforward sense legal, but has more the nature of exhortation or persuasion: motive clauses, in fact.

What I have in mind are 'asides' like the following:

Ex. 22.21: 'You shall not wrong an alien or oppress him, for you were aliens in the land of Egypt. You shall not afflict any widow or orphan. If you do afflict them, and they cry out to me, I will surely hear their cry; and my wrath will burn, and I will kill you with the sword, and your wives shall become widows and your children fatherless.'

Ex. 22.26–27: 'If ever you take your neighbour's garment in pledge, you shall restore it to him before the sun goes down; for that is his only covering, it is his mantle for his body; in what else shall he sleep? And if he cries to me, I will hear, for I am compassionate.'

Ex. 23.7–8: 'Keep far from a false charge, and do not slay the innocent and righteous, for I will not acquit the wicked. And you shall take no bribe, for a bribe blinds the officials, and subverts the cause of those who are in the right.'

Ex. 23.9: 'You shall not oppress an alien; you know the heart of an alien, for you were aliens in the land of Egypt.'

The motivations for good conduct here are of various kinds. Doing wrong to aliens, it is suggested in the first and last passages just quoted, should be ruled out by two considerations. The first is the fact that Israelites know what it is like to be an alien – which makes the principle of good behaviour towards immigrants a subset of the so-called Golden Rule, Do not do to others what you would not like them to do to you. The second is a declaration by God that he will personally avenge misconduct towards aliens – a divine threat. One might suspect that it was particularly hard to get people to act in a kindly way towards resident aliens, just as it is today in many societies (certainly in Britain). Maybe the divine sanctions are also invoked because of the comparative vagueness of the law. We do not know exactly what would have amounted to 'oppressing' an alien, and much of it might have been difficult to punish through the legal system. So, rather than appoint a penalty, offenders are threatened with divine action. The very inclusion of this kind of rule, which is so difficult to define or enforce, may already hint that the Book of the Covenant is more than a legal code.

Motivation through threats also appears in the law

about widows and orphans. It was usual in the ancient Near East to present one or other of the gods as the defender of these people, who had so few legal rights in the societies of ancient times. In Israel Yahweh naturally took on this function. People are warned against exploiting widows and orphans through a reminder that Yahweh is their protector. Since he threatens to punish offenders 'with the sword', presumably some human tribunal is envisaged, though we are not told how this will operate. The tit-for-tat character of the punishment – 'your wife shall be a widow and your children fatherless' – is very common in the Old Testament, and its appeal to some kind of natural sense that the punishment should fit the crime seems to me to align it with a natural law ethic.[1]

The same is perhaps true of the law about pledges. In ancient Israel it was evidently possible to pawn one's possessions for money, but in general the law does not regulate the practice. Here, however, we're dealing with the limiting case, where the poor person pawns the last thing he has, his outer cloak, which served him as a coat by day but as bedclothes by night. If he is reduced that far, it is enacted that the pledge-taker shall restore the garment in the evening – presumably, each evening – so that he shall not freeze. Here again the law is concerned not with the normal case but with the extreme, and requires a kind of benevolence, not simply justice. But it is interesting to see the motivation offered, which is similar to that for the law on widows and orphans: first, an appeal to common sense or natural sympathy for the sufferer – 'after all, that is his garment, what else is he supposed to sleep in?' – which brooks no disagreement; and then, secondly, a threat of divine intervention, based on the premise that Yahweh is merciful in a way that men, often, are not.

The law about perverting the course of justice follows the same route. Yahweh will not acquit those who condemn the innocent because they have been bribed to do so, and fear of his vengeance should dissuade them. But so should a consideration of the nature of the case. Bribes should be avoided not only because they risk divine punishment, but also because they are inherently wrong, since they lead to those who administer justice 'blinding their own eyes' (turning a blind eye, as we say) and thus acting perversely. This is said as though it is quite obvious that perverting justice is wrong, something that all reasonable people would agree about. The motivation is thus subtler than a threat of punishment; it is an appeal to a common moral sense. Again, it aligns itself more with natural than with positive law, and rests on a moral consensus which the author can take for granted, or believes that he can.

Perhaps it is time to make what I want to say about the motivation of Old Testament law rather more formal, and to draw some maps of the different kind of motives that we find. Some of the motive clauses look back in time – this is especially true of the appeal to the knowledge of the 'heart of an alien' that the Israelites acquired in Egypt – while others look forward, in fear of a possible punishment by Yahweh but (in texts we have not yet examined) also in hope of a reward from him. Gratitude and fear are both possible motivations for conduct, and one is backward-, the other forward-looking. To complete the picture (though this may seem slightly more contrived) we could describe the appeal to the inherent rightness of the law as a motivation based on the present. You should do this or that because its rightness should appeal to you, or to your better nature; acting like this will give you the satisfaction of doing what you should, whether or not there is any future reward beyond the act itself. If we can accept this classification at least provisionally, then we have a basic map of ethical motivation based on a scheme of past, present, and future, on which we can plot the positions taken up in various Old Testament books.

1. Future Motivations

The last of these, motivation based on the future, seems to me the most common device for encouraging good conduct in the Old Testament. The world of Old Testament ethics is very much a world of sticks and carrots, threatening punishment for sin and promising blessing for righteousness. Both elements are already present in the Ten Commandments, the stick in the commandment against graven images ('You shall not bow down to them or serve them, for I the LORD your God am a jealous God, visiting the iniquity of the fathers upon the children'), the carrot in the commandment about honouring parents which is, as the author of Ephesians puts it (6.2) 'the first commandment with a promise': 'Honour your father and your mother, that your days may be long in the land which the LORD your God gives you.' Of all the books of the law, Deuteronomy probably develops this theme most, and it can be seen in the remarkable passage in Deut. 10–11 in which Moses exhorts and cajoles the people to try to make them obedient to God's commandments (this is a passage to which I will return). The people are exhorted to take on a purity appropriate to the God they serve, and this is expressed in the strange image of the 'circumcision of the heart', found also in Jeremiah (4.4). 'Circumcise therefore the foreskin of your heart,' Moses says, 'and be no longer stubborn. For the LORD your God is God of gods and Lord of lords, the great, the mighty, and the terrible God, who is not partial and takes no bribe' (Deut. 10.16). God's justice cannot be bought off; hence he is to be feared more even than a human judge, for there are often ways of circumventing judges on earth, but with God there can be no negotiation.

But in Deuteronomy at least promise tends to predominate over threat, as in the lengthy passage that follows (11.8–15):

'You shall therefore keep all the commandment which I command you this day, that you may be strong, and go in and take possession of the land which you are going over to possess, and that you may live long in the land which the LORD swore to your fathers to give to them and to their descendants, a land flowing with milk and honey. For the land which you are entering to take possession of it is not like the land of Egypt, from which you have come, where you sowed your seed and watered it with your feet, like a garden of vegetables; but the land which you are going over to possess is a land of hills and valleys, which drinks water by the rain from heaven, and land which the LORD your God cares for; for the eyes of the LORD your God are always upon it, from the beginning of the year to the end of the year.

'And if you will obey my commandments which I command you this day, to love the LORD your God, and to serve him with all your heart and with all your soul, he will give the rain for your land in its season, the early rain and the later rain, that you may gather in your grain and your wine and your oil. And he will give grass in your fields for your cattle, and you shall eat and be full.'

The idea that well-doing brings a divine blessing, wrong-doing a divine curse, seems to have been wholly uncontroversial in the world Israel inhabited. It is present just as much in the prophets as in the law: Isaiah says, 'If you are willing and obedient, you shall eat the good of the land, but if you refuse and rebel, you shall be devoured by the sword' (1.19–20). Indeed the prophetic message of coming judgment as a punishment for national sin makes no sense unless there was a general assumption in the culture that God punishes sinners but rewards the righteous. The prophets do not spend any time trying to convince their audience that that is how things are, presumably because they accepted it without question. What they do have to spend time on is the task of persuading their hearers that they are in fact guilty, not innocent: in other words, that this agreed principle has the logical consequence that they will receive divine punishment, since they deserve it. In the nature of the case the pre-exilic prophets at least do not seem to utter many conditional promises, since they are convinced that it is already too late for most of their hearers to change their conduct in a way that would lead to divine favour. But they spend many words on threats, trying to convince people that disaster will follow unless they change their ways, or even that the time for a change is now so long past that only disaster lies before them. The assumption that conduct can be motivated by an appeal to the future is taken for granted by them all.

This is equally obvious if we turn to the wisdom tradition, where Proverbs insists (often against the evidence) that good things come to good people, evil things to evil ones:

My son, do not forget my teaching,
but let your heart keep my commandments;
for length of days and years of life
and abundant welfare will they give you.

Let not loyalty and faithfulness forsake you;
bind them about your neck,
write them on the tablet of your heart.
So you will find favour and good repute
in the sight of God and man.

Trust in the LORD with all your heart,
and do not rely on your own insight.
In all your ways acknowledge him,
and he will make straight your paths.
Be not wise in your own eyes;
fear the LORD, and turn away from evil.
It will be healing to your flesh
and refreshment to your bones (3.1–8).

The prevalence of these ideas in wisdom writings is a

reminder that they do not occur only where ethics is understood as divine commandment. Where that *is* the understanding, as in much of the Pentateuch, then certainly God is seen as the one who rewards or punishes the keeping or breaking of his commandments. But in the wisdom literature, where on the whole a theory much more like what we have been calling natural law predominates, there is just as much insistence on the outcome of human conduct in prosperity or disaster. Indeed, for writers who thought in terms of the natural consequences of conduct rather than of divine decisions to bless or curse, the nexus between conduct and result may have been even tighter than for those, like the prophets, who wanted to stress the divine will as the cause of what befalls men and women. German scholarship has dubbed this link the 'act-consequence relationship' (*der Tun-Ergehen-Zusammenhang*), to emphasize the sense we get from wisdom writers that the consequences of an action for good or ill are somehow bound up with the action itself, and come about more or less automatically. If the matter is seen like this, then there is hardly a gap between willing an action and willing its consequences: it is not an open question whether good or ill will result from doing this or that, but a foregone conclusion.

It is this sense that we always know in advance that good behaviour will lead to prosperity and bad behaviour to adversity which produces the somewhat dogmatic character of wisdom literature, so offensive to many modern readers. The so-called wisdom psalm, Psalm 37, takes these ideas to their logical conclusion in v. 25: 'I have been young, and now am old; yet I have not seen the righteous forsaken, or his children begging bread', inviting the rejoinder, 'You obviously don't get out enough.' But this is not really an empirical observation, though it is, conventionally, cast in the form of one; it is a statement of dogmatic principle. And it is a statement that many of those who contributed to the Old Testament would have agreed with, but which most thoughtful people today find largely unacceptable.

Ethical motivation by reference to the future is in fact so common in the Old Testament that it might lead us to a rather surprising conclusion. Just as it has been normal to treat Old Testament ethics as a case, even the paradigm case, of positive rather than of natural law, so it has been usual to see ethics in the Bible as a particularly clear example of a 'deontological' approach (i.e. an approach based on the idea of duty or obligation). The Old Testament, that is to say, lays down what people should or should not do; it does not suggest what are the best ways of attaining a certain goal – say, happiness. To put it another way, the Old Testament does not present a 'teleological' approach to ethics, one concerned with ends and goods, with the goal human beings set themselves; it is interested only in what people *ought* to do. But as with the alleged predominance of positive law, so with the account of Old Testament ethics as deontological I would like to suggest that matters are not as simple as they seem.

One interesting, though not necessarily all-important, factor is that biblical Hebrew lacks any clear way of expressing deontological modality. There is no Hebrew verb that we can translate 'ought', a fact that made it strange for Walter Eichrodt in his *Theology of the Old*

Testament to take 'the Unconditional Ought' as the central point for his discussion of morality in the Old Testament.[2] Obligation is conveyed either by an imperative or related forms like the cohortative or jussive, or by a simple future – the latter especially after negatives, hence the familiar translation of the Ten Commandments, 'Thou shalt not steal', and so on. Nevertheless linguistic arguments of this kind are never completely satisfactory, and it can be argued that Hebrew has adequate resources for conveying 'oughtness', even if by long periphrases.

Much more important is the observation that the possibility of good conduct unmotivated by the expectation of future benefit is in fact very rare in Old Testament texts. The only clear instances I can think of occur in two of the later books, Job and Daniel. In the prologue to Job, the Satan asks God, 'Does Job fear God for nothing?' He suggests that Job's piety is self-serving: 'Put forth thy hand, and touch all that he has, and he will curse thee to thy face' (Job 1.11). In the event, the Satan turns out to be wrong, because Job stands by his piety whatever happens to him, ascribing the glory to God even when he is deprived of all his goods, of his whole family except his wife, and finally even of his own health. But the question is raised of whether someone could be pious even though he or she had no reward for it, as though this was an important question, and in the end disinterested piety is shown to be possible, even if only in the case of a very exceptional person. (I disregard here the verse dialogue in Job, where a very different Job emerges.)

In Daniel disinterestedness arises in the case of the three young men thrown into the burning fiery furnace for refusing to worship the image that Nebuchadnezzar has set up (Dan. 3). They first assert that their God, the God of Israel, is well able to deliver them from the king's power, and that he will in fact do so; but they continue, 'but if not, be it known to you, O king, that we will not serve your gods or worship the image that you have set up' (Dan. 3.18). Commentators generally interpret the three young men as symbols of the Maccabean martyrs, those who died at the hands of the pagan king Antiochus IV Epiphanes in the second century BC for insisting on remaining loyal to Jewish customs and refusing to assimilate to Hellenistic practices. This would make good sense, since there too the lack of any apparent reward for such piety was a problem. It is often said, though, that Jewish belief in the resurrection of the dead sprang from this situation, as a way of asserting that God would indeed vindicate and reward his faithful servants even beyond the death which the tyrant inflicted on them. In Daniel 3, however, nothing is said of any such possible reward, and the three young men are presented as representatives of a wholly disinterested piety, just like the Job of the prose sections of the book of Job.

But these two examples are all I can find.[3] For the most part the Old Testament takes it for granted that people pursue the good for the sake of an end. That end may be presented as material prosperity, as it is in Deuteronomy, or as the more subtle satisfaction of life with God, as in some of the Psalms – e.g. Psalm 73. But it is not usual to think of there being no goal, as though God or nature makes demands on people but makes no return. There is a Christian hymn that runs:

My God, I love thee; not because
   I hope for heaven thereby,
Nor yet because who love thee not
   Are lost eternally.

I think that most of the authors of the Old Testament could have understood this, in a theoretical way, and clearly the authors of Job and Daniel had reflected on this kind of problem. But most of them would not have thought it a very sensible attitude. Life with God is a partnership, and in it there is give and take: God does not do all the taking and we all the giving. A teleological element in ethics seemed simply common sense to ancient Israelites, who acted so as to obey God, of course, but in the belief that he had promised good things to those who did obey him and threatened with misfortune those who left his ways. To say that we should be moral, but not for the sake of gaining anything, would have struck them as an unrealistic refinement of piety.

2. Past motivations

In speaking of motivation by reference to the past I mostly have in mind the idea that moral conduct should spring from gratitude to God. This is a common theme in both Old and New Testaments. Moral conduct is motivated by saying that we should be moral because we owe it to God, it should spring from our gratitude to him. We could of course respond: Yes, but why should we be grateful? How is gratitude itself motivated or justified? But the Old Testament does not deal with that question, regarding the obligation to be grateful for kindnesses received as self-evident – perhaps in effect as one of those obligations that belong to the natural law. We do not find Old Testament writers who think that they have to go beyond or behind the obligation to be grateful. Once they have said that Israel should act morally because of what God has done for them, they are content to leave it at that.

A classic example of the appeal to gratitude for what God has done can be found, again, in Deut. 10–11:

> 'And now, Israel, what does the LORD your God require of you, but to fear the LORD your God, to walk in all his ways, to love him, to serve the LORD your God with all your heart and with all your soul, and to keep the commandments and statutes of the LORD, which I command you this day for your good? Behold, to the LORD your God belong heaven and the heaven of heavens, the earth with all that is in it; yet the LORD set his heart in love upon your fathers and chose their descendants after them, you above all peoples, as at this day . . . You shall fear the LORD your God; you shall serve him and cleave to him, and by his name you shall swear. He is your praise; he is your God, who has done for you these great and terrible things which your eyes have seen. Your fathers went down to Egypt seventy persons; and now the LORD your God has made you as the stars of heaven for multitude' (Deut. 10.12–15, 20–22).

The laws God gives are to be obeyed, not simply because he gives them, but because he has a claim on his people, arising from the good he has done them in the past. This is an equally common idea in the prophets, where Israel is continually castigated for ingratitude, as in the famous text from Micah which is the source of the Reproaches used in the Western liturgical tradition on Good Friday. 'O my people, what have I done to you? In what have I wearied you? Answer me! For I brought you up from the land of Egypt, and redeemed you from the house of bondage; and I sent before you Moses, Aaron, and Miriam' (Micah 6.3–4). Compare also the haunting lament in Isa. 63.7–64.12, probably contemporary with the book of Lamentations, in other words from the early sixth century when Jerusalem fell to the Babylonians:

> He said, Surely they are my people, sons who will not deal falsely; and he became their Saviour. In all their affliction he was afflicted,[4] and the angel of his presence saved them; in his love and in his pity he redeemed them; he lifted them up and carried them all the days of old. But they rebelled and grieved his Holy Spirit (63.8–10).

The idea of obedience springing from gratitude as the basis of moral conduct is fundamental to a great deal of the Old Testament. Indeed, it is probably only in the earlier wisdom literature that it is wholly lacking. It lies at the root of the covenant, which is a contract between Yahweh and Israel predicated on the prior act of salvation by Yahweh which gives him a claim on Israel's attention and loyalty. Within texts dealing with the covenant, it is true, we find an appeal to desired future prosperity alongside the reminder of Yahweh's past kindness. This is particularly true in Deuteronomy, which is the Old Testament's covenant text par excellence. But the logic of Deuteronomy's quite complex presentation is that Israel should obey Yahweh first and foremost because of what he has already done for them, and then secondarily in the expectation of receiving further blessings. The line of thinking runs: You are in a special relationship with Yahweh which did not arise from your own effort or merit, and you should obey him out of gratitude. Nevertheless bear in mind that what he freely created he can freely destroy, and be careful to remain in loyal submission to him, so that the covenant relationship may continue as happily in the future as it did in the past.

There is some importance in establishing that gratitude is (or is meant to be) prior to motivation by expected future benefits, because this has a bearing on the interpretation of various New Testament texts. One of the great achievements of the New Testament scholar E. P. Sanders has been to correct the impression often given in studies of Paul that the Judaism of Paul's day was a religion of bargaining with God, serving God for the sake of the benefits he would confer – and, conversely, believing that God's blessing depended on human obedience to him. This is what generations of Christians have thought of as 'Pharisaism', an ungenerous religion in which you have to do good works before God will take any notice of you – a religion, in fact, in which salvation has to be earned. Sanders has shown that Paul's Jewish contemporaries would have been just as horrified at such an idea of God's covenant with Israel as any modern Christian.[5] If such an idea of true religion did have to be combated in the early church, it must have come into existence as an inner-Christian distortion, because it was certainly not to be found in Judaism. For Jews, it was axiomatic that God's choice of Israel preceded any good works that Israel might perform: as Deuteronomy puts it, 'The LORD your God is not giving you this good land to possess because of your righteousness; for you are a stubborn people' (Deut. 9.6). Many commandments were indeed laid upon Israel, but they were a consequence of Yahweh's love, not a precondition of it. Jews believed, just as Paul did, that there were very stringent demands made by God of the people of God, but they were not the conditions on which he would be prepared to bless them; they were, rather, the way they could show gratitude to him for his entirely free love of them. As Deuteronomy stresses, obedience to the laws is very little to ask in comparison with what God has done for Israel: 'what does the LORD your God require of you, but to fear the LORD your God, to walk in all his ways, to love him, to serve the LORD your God with all your heart and with all your soul, and to keep the commandments of the LORD, which I command you today for your good?' (Deut. 10.12–13).

3. Present motivation

This leads us naturally to the third kind of motivation for ethical behaviour: what I have called motivation in the present. When Deuteronomy claims that the laws the Israelites are obliged to obey are for their own good, this amounts to saying that moral behaviour is more desirable in itself than immoral: it is an advantage to have, and to keep, the sort of laws that God has given to Israel. Keeping the law should be a delight in itself. This is not quite the same as the attitude that thinks no motivation is needed, as

in Daniel and Job, though it comes close. Rather, it thinks
that there *is* a reward for well-doing, but that this is
inherent in living a law-abiding life, and makes the
well-doer happy even if there are no external benefits.
Deuteronomy is quite explicit about this: 'Behold, I have
taught you statutes and ordinances, as the LORD my God
commanded me, that you should do them in the land
which you are entering to take possession of it. Keep them
and do them; for that will be your wisdom and your
understanding in the sight of the peoples, who, when they
hear all these statutes, will say, "Surely this great nation is
a wise and understanding people." For what great nation
is there that has a god so near to it as the LORD our God is
to us, whenever we call upon him? And what great nation
is there, that has statutes and ordinances so righteous as all
this law which I set before you this day?' (Deut. 4.5–8).

But the chief place where we find this kind of motivation
for keeping the law, based on its inherent beauty and per-
fection, is the Psalter. The most obvious example of it is in
Psalm 19: 'The law of the LORD is perfect, reviving the
soul; the testimony of the LORD is sure, making wise the
simple; the precepts of the LORD are right, rejoicing the
heart; the commandment of the LORD is pure, enlightening
the eyes; the fear of the LORD is clean, enduring for ever;
the ordinances of the LORD are true, and righteous alto-
gether. More to be desired are they than gold, even much
fine gold; sweeter also than honey, and drippings of the
honeycomb' (Ps. 19.7–10). And Psalm 119, all 176 verses
of it, develops what we could call a spirituality of the
Torah, in which contemplation of the beauty of God's laws
becomes almost a path to a mystical experience: 'I opened

my mouth, and drew in my breath, because I longed for thy commandments' (Ps. 119.131, my translation); 'I rejoice at thy word like one who finds great spoils' (v. 162).

C. S. Lewis wrote an excellent chapter about this law-mysticism in his *Reflections on the Psalms*,[6] and pointed to one of its finest and most sympathetic expressions in literature outside the Jewish tradition, in Racine's tragedy *Athalie (Athaliah)*, where at the end of Act 1 the chorus of young girls of the tribe of Levi sings a hymn in praise of the law which contains the wonderful line 'O divine, ô charmante loi', 'O divine, O charming law'!– 'desirable', I suppose, would be better than 'charming'. It goes on to speak of the joy of serving God by keeping his command-ments, for 'il nous donne ses loix, il se donne luy-même' – 'he gives us his laws, he gives us himself'. It is indeed *by* giving us the law that God gives us himself: the law is the form God takes when he makes himself known to us. It is not surprising that some early Christians seem to have developed a law christology: if God was to be encountered in Christ, then he must be, in some sense, identical with the Torah, for that was where God was to be encountered. This implies a very high valuation of the expressed will of God as the way by which people are meant to live, and which will be their whole and only good, whatever conse-quences may or may not follow.

Conclusion

In this chapter I have tried to show how the Old Testament motivates moral conduct and answers the question, 'Why should we be moral?' Despite the intricacy of some of the positions I have examined, they can be mapped on to a simple scheme of past, present and future as the point of reference from which motivation is derived. Although it does not think philosophically, the Old Testament does use what may be called quasi-philosophical lines of thought in trying to give its readers adequate reasons for acting morally: it is far from relying simply on assertion or diktat.

And this might be said generally of the topics examined in this book. Of course we have to allow for the fact that the Old Testament comes to us from a remote and alien culture, and one which had not yet developed the sophisticated powers of philosophical analysis which we owe to the Greeks. Yet when we do so, we at once find that what we encounter in the Old Testament is far from being simply unphilosophical; still less, crude and clumsy. Some powerful minds worked on most of the books the Old Testament contains, and in the ethical sphere they had things to say which remain evocative and suggestive for our own moral enquiries. I've consistently tried to avoid bringing in theological beliefs about the inspiration of these documents, because I have wanted to let them speak on their own terms; and, though this naturally prevents me from now claiming that they ought to have a greater authority and status for us today than, for example, the major works of classical antiquity such as the plays of the great Greek tragedians or the philosophy of Plato and Aristotle, I hope to have suggested reasons for thinking that they are at least in the same league. They deserve our close and sympathetic attention as we go about trying to work out our own account of what it is to lead a moral life.

Notes

1. The Vitality of Old Testament Ethics

1. Andrew Brown in the *Church Times*, 15 November 1996.
2. Martha C. Nussbaum, *The Fragility of Goodness: Luck and Ethics in Greek Tragedy and Philosophy*, CUP 1986.
3. Martha C. Nussbaum, *Love's Knowledge: Essays on Philosophy and Literature*, OUP 1990.
4. *The Fragility of Goodness*, p.505. The reference is to Aristotle's *Nicomachean Ethics*.

2. Ethics and Story

1. See Stanley E. Hauerwas, *The Peaceable Kingdom*, SCM Press 1984 and University of Notre Dame Press 1983.
2. *The Fragility of Goodness*, pp.300f.
3. No doubt the fact that Hauerwas is concerned with God as in some sense the author is bound to mean that for him the 'plot' is central, as it cannot be for Nussbaum who has no theological commitment. I am grateful to my colleague David Reimer for pointing this out.

4. There is an extended discussion of the various possibilities here in Meir Sternberg, *The Poetics of Biblical Literature*, Indiana University Press 1985.
5. See *Love's Knowledge*, pp. 354–55.

3. Three Ethical Issues

1. See Phyllis Trible, *Texts of Terror*, SCM Press 1992 and Fortress Press 1984.

4. Divine Commands or Natural Law?

1. See James Barr, *Biblical Faith and Natural Theology* (The Gifford Lectures for 1991), Clarendon Press 1993.
2. W. C. Spohn, *What are they saying about Scripture and Ethics?*, Paulist Press, New York 1984, pp. 36–53.
3. See John Barton, *Amos' Oracles against the Nations*, CUP 1980.
4. See H. H. Schmid, *Wesen und Geschichte der Weisheit. Eine Untersuchung zur altorientalischen und israelitischen Weisheitsliteratur*, Berlin 1966.
5. M. Douglas, *Purity and Danger: An Analysis of Concepts of Pollution and Taboo*, Penguin Books 1970.

5. Why Should we be Moral?

1. See John Barton, 'Natural Law and Poetic Justice in the Old Testament', *Journal of Theological Studies* 30 (1979), pp. 1–14.

Notes

2. Walter Eichrodt, *Theology of the Old Testament*, Vol. 2, SCM Press and Westminster Press 1967, pp. 316–79.

3. Though there is also a suggestion of disinterested piety in Hab. 3.17–18:

> Though the fig tree do not blossom,
>   nor fruit be on the vines,
> the produce of the olive fail
>   and the fields yield no food,
> the flock be cut off from the fold
>   and there be no herd in the stalls,
> yet I will rejoice in the LORD,
>   I will joy in the God of my salvation.

I am grateful to my colleague David Reimer for suggesting that this passage should be included.

4. The meaning of the text is obscure here, and recent translations prefer 'he became their Saviour in all their afflictions' (thus NRSV).

5. See E. P. Sanders, *Paul and Palestinian Judaism*, SCM Press and Fortress Press 1977 and *Paul, the Law, and the Jewish People*, SCM Press and Fortress Press 1985.

6. C. S. Lewis, *Reflections on the Psalms*, Fontana 1958, pp. 49–57.